W. L. Engu...

Seattle

April 20, 1928

S H Scudder
1951

ART OF THE NIGHT

THE WORKS OF
GEORGE JEAN NATHAN

THE AUTOBIOGRAPHY OF AN ATTITUDE

THE AMERICAN CREDO (*Vols. I and II in collaboration with H. L. Mencken*)

THE NEW AMERICAN CREDO

THE WORLD IN FALSEFACE

THE HOUSE OF SATAN

LAND OF THE PILGRIMS' PRIDE

EUROPE AFTER 8:15 (*in collaboration with Mencken*)

THE POPULAR THEATRE

MR. GEORGE JEAN NATHAN PRESENTS

COMEDIANS ALL

ANOTHER BOOK ON THE THEATRE

THE THEATRE, THE DRAMA, THE GIRLS

MATERIA CRITICA

THE CRITIC AND THE DRAMA

A BOOK WITHOUT A TITLE

BOTTOMS UP

HELIOGABALUS (*in collaboration with Mencken*)

ART OF THE NIGHT

IN COLLABORATIVE COMPILATIONS

A PORTFOLIO OF AMERICAN EDITORS, *edited by Louis Evan Shipman*
CIVILIZATION IN THE UNITED STATES, *edited by Harold Stearns*

PREFACES

THE MOON OF THE CARIBBEES AND OTHER PLAYS, *by Eugene O'Neill*
CHICAGO, *by Maurine Watkins*
TWELVE THOUSAND, *by Bruno Frank*

BOOKS ON MR. NATHAN

THE THEATRE OF GEORGE JEAN NATHAN, *by Isaac Goldberg, Ph. D.*
PISTOLS FOR TWO, *by Owen Hatteras*

ART OF THE NIGHT

GEORGE JEAN NATHAN

ALFRED · A · KNOPF
NEW YORK 1928 *LONDON*

CONTENTS

ART OF THE NIGHT

ADVICE TO A YOUNG CRITIC

§ 1

The greatest weakness of the average critic is his wish to be more than critic. He somehow believes that, however capable he may be as a critic, there is a call for him to demonstrate his talent in fields removed from criticism if he would augment and solidify his standing in his profession. We thus find critics as novelists, playwrights, producers, poets, biographers, husbands and what not, striving to support their critical position by achievements in extrinsic directions. For they imagine that they will be regarded as greater critics if they prove that they can do something apart from criticism, however dubious the quality of their performances. They shrink nervously from the charge that they are merely critics and not what are known as creative fellows. All this has led and leads to a deterioration of criticism, for the simple reason

1

that criticism worth its salt is a job quite sufficient unto itself and calling upon its practitioner's
fullest time and resources.

The art of criticism is too often looked upon as
a mere prelude and stepping-stone to a practice of
one of the other arts, when it should be regarded
—as, of course, it is by those sufficiently familiar with it in its finest flower—as an art of itself and a thing apart. The good critic has earned
his right to reward by being a good critic. If he
happens also to be something of a genius and succeeds as well in some other art, he deserves a
doubled reward, of course. But, in the general run
of things, he should be content to be what he is,
a critic first and last, and leave to other men the
jobs that they in turn should content themselves
with.

§ 2

If you have violent prejudices, do not be afraid
of them. Give them a free course. Do not be dis-
quieted because they seem to be at variance with
the convictions of other critics. Few things are absolutely true in this world and you stand as good

a chance of being right as the next man. Only exercise a caution never to be indignant and always to smile. In the event that it turns out that you have been wrong—even to the extent of being idiotic— you will thus be safe, for most persons will conclude that you were just fooling and will secretly be a bit abashed for having fallen into your trap.

§ 3

If you are accused of arbitrarily adopting a *contra mundum* attitude, don't lose any sleep over it. Nine-tenths of the world's greatest men achieved greatness by arbitrarily opposing the convictions and beliefs of the majority. The criticism of you might just as aptly have been directed against Christ, Galileo, Columbus, Voltaire, Pasteur, Mergenthaler and the Wrights—if, after you have confected some ephemeral little destructive essay on John Drinkwater or the movies, that gives you any comfort.

§ 4

Take your work seriously, but not yourself. Fifty years hence, your work may prove to have

3

amounted to something. Fifty years hence, on the other hand, you will have been eaten by the same indiscriminating worms that found Clement Scott and Acton Davies such appetizing delicatessen.

§ 5

Don't be afraid to dissent from the opinions of the critically great. Remember that Nietzsche considered Kotzebue a more talented dramatist than Schiller, that Hazlitt placed Foote and O'Keeffe among the immortals and called the latter the English Molière, that Dryden declared that Fletcher came nearer to perfection in comedy than Shakespeare, that both Lessing and Diderot considered George Lillo a model dramatist, that George Bernard Shaw thinks Brieux the greatest living dramatic writer this side of Russia, and that William Archer once actually observed (*vide* "The Theatrical World of 1895," pg. 271) that he venerated Mr. Augustus Thomas' "Alabama" so highly that he wished it would be published in book form so that he might go around quoting it!

4

§ 6

I need not tell you, obviously enough, that morals have no place in any consideration of art. But do not make a fool of yourself when the point comes to issue, as so many critics are in the habit of doing. The latter often make themselves as ridiculous in their way as the moralists do in theirs. If the question before the house is one of authentic art, that is, if the work criticized is of genuine artistic integrity and if the question of its morality is interposed by meddling smutsers, let fly at the dolts with full artillery. But if the work criticized has no artistic justification and integrity, don't make yourself silly by defending it with the same arguments used in the former case. There is such a thing as art, and it should be held sacred and inviolate from the assaults of dirty-minded morons; but there is also such a thing as cheap smut, and it should be frankly admitted to be just that and nothing more. Certain critics, however, having established themselves in full feather as tomahawkers of all moral interference with anything, lack all discrimination when moral issues are raised and rush to the defence of Cabell and Mae West with one and the same argument. They grow as excited over the moral assault upon out-and-out dung like "Sex" as they do over the moral assault upon a first-rate piece of work like "Jurgen." And, in so doing, they weaken their case—a case that must be kept strong at all costs and one that needs the fighting brains of all intelligent critics—and give the enemy certain points of advantage in the minds of liberal and rational men. After all, there is a difference between "A Night in a Turkish Harem" and even Brieux's "Damaged Goods," and to defend the former in terms of the latter is like having a drink with the colored gentleman who has defiled your sister.

§ 7

Do not confound an aphrodisiacal actress with a talented one. The majority of critics do so, and, I regret to confess it, understandably and even a bit justifiably. If an actress stimulates your libido, say so frankly and do not try to conceal the truth in a lot of rigmarole about histrionic art. There is certainly nothing wrong with an actress who has sex appeal; indeed, it is five times more valuable to her and to a liberal portion of her art than all the stock company training this side of Cleveland and Rochester; and even if the professors object to what you write, the girl herself, I venture to say, will be tickled to death. . . . You will note, if you take the trouble to investigate, that all the more profound treatises on the art of acting are and have been written by grandpas, valetudinarians or favorites of the celebrated Dowager Empress Tsen Hi.

§ 8

The better and more honest critic you are, the fewer friends will eventually send flowers up to the funeral parlor. One by one they will soon or late withdraw from fellowship and good will. Even one's closest friend cannot abide criticism of himself with half the fortitude and amiability of one's worst enemy. Show me a critic with a quorum of artists as bosom comrades and I'll show you a critic who is a hypocrite and a liar.

7

§ 9

Pay no attention to what people say or write of you. A man in the brick-throwing business must expect occasionally to be hit by a brick.

§ 10

To be a critic automatically implies a certain self-sufficiency and vanity. Never mind. You will never find an artist among the diffident and submissive. Genuine artistic expression, in whatever field, calls for a forthright faith and confidence. It took more nerve and downright courage to write the "Essay on Morals" than it took to fight Waterloo.

§ 11

Never fall into the error of believing that simply because a thing is unpopular it must have esoteric points of merit. Vastly more trash fails to win popular approval than wins it. If Rostand's "The Last Night of Don Juan" runs only a week in the American theatre, remember that John J. Hack's "One Glorious Hour" doesn't run even that long.

And if "Abie's Irish Rose" runs for five years, stop and reflect that "Hamlet" will run for five thousand.

§ 12

Don't be afraid of being labeled a destructive critic. You will be in good company. Where would you rather be: in Hell with Swift, Voltaire and Nietzsche or in the American Academy of Arts and Letters with Richard Burton, Clayton Hamilton and Hermann Hagedorn?

§ 13

Since you are an American, write like an American. Do not try to become a member of the Charles Lamb's Club and ape the so-called literary manner of the English critical essayists. Express yourself in the pungent idiom of your time, your land and your people; there is no apology necessary; that idiom may produce sound literature as well as the language of the dons. Don't be afraid of slang if it will make your point better and more forcibly than literose expression. Much that was erstwhile slang has already been accepted into the

9

dictionaries of formal English; much more will be accepted in the near future. The objection to slang, at least to the more valid slang, is snooty and snobbish. Where a more expressive word or phrase in the language than *to cuckoo* (in the sense of *to imitate*), *sap, to get away with, bonehead, wow, to razz, joy-juice* (for *gin*), *to vamp, hickpricker, joy-ride* or *hoopla?* But, on the other hand, don't make the mistake of believing that a mere imitation of Brook, Indiana, will get you any farther than an imitation of Cambridge, England.

§ 14

It is as absurd to believe that the general public is interested in sound dramatic criticism as it is to believe that the general public is interested in sound drama. It is to the credit of the majority of newspaper editors that they appreciate the fact and take pains not to discommode their readers.

§ 15

There is, at bottom, very little difference between dramatic criticism and literary criticism.

What, after all, is a play but an underwritten novel and a novel but an overwritten play?

§ 16

The chief fault with many critics is that they strive to divert to themselves the attention, if any, that their criticism should attract to itself.

§ 17

One of the worst curses that American dramatic criticism has suffered is the Shaw influence. Twenty years ago, there wasn't a young critic, myself included, who didn't in one way or another reflect the Shaw attitude, viewpoint and manner. Since that time, the influence has faded somewhat, but it is still sufficiently in evidence to be immediately recognizable. Shaw, surely, was a stimulatingly excellent critic and worse deities might have been and might still be picked out to emulate. But one wonders if the young men who still regard him as their critical *beau idéal* really appreciate the gaping holes in his dramatic taste and judgment. If they will take the trouble to read carefully his two volumes of "Dramatic Opinions and Essays," they may be rather alarmed and flabbergasted to find out that among the plays and the dramatists he selected for a share of his admiration were the following: "The Prude's Progress," B. C. Stephenson, H. V. Esmond's "The Divided Way," W. Yardley, "The Strange Adventures of Miss Brown," W. D. Howells' "A Dangerous Ruffian," "Mrs. Ponderbury's Past," "The Romance of the Shop-Walker," Miss Clo Graves' "Mother of Three," and W. G. Wills' "Olivia." As for his judgment of actors, they will perhaps be equally flustered to observe that he ranked Joseph Jefferson with Coquelin and Salvini. As for his estimate of dramatic literature, they will be somewhat shocked to encounter this: "Nobody ever could, or did, or will improve on Dumas' . . . plays." And as for his style, they may be dismayed to find him resorting to such clichés of present-day Hearst critical writing as *Amurrican* and the *long-lost chee-yild*.

§ 18

All criticism, after all, is a criticism of the critic himself before it is one of the criticized.

12

§ 19

The reason why there are so few good farces written in America is that the farce form is sneered at, or at least treated with an air of condescension, by nine-tenths of the men who write about the native theatre. This is particularly true, strangely enough, of critics who are otherwise competent and discerning fellows. Yet these, like the general run of ignoramuses, indirectly discourage our more capable dramatists from essaying farce by treating it as something more or less negligible. When these writers think of farce, they think of such things as "Charley's Aunt," "The Man From Mexico," and "The Strawberry Blonde," but for some reason or other they seem never to stop and think of such others as "The Frogs," "Le Bourgeois Gentilhomme" and "The Comedy of Errors."

§ 20

The bulk of American criticism is corrupted by a blind adherence to and championing of favorites. There is hardly a critic in practice amongst us who hasn't a pet artist who, in his estimation, can do no wrong. Having once set the artist in question atop a pedestal, the critic is determined by hook or crook to keep him there, even though the fellow's work be periodically anything but sound and meritorious. The critic seems to imagine that such slips on the part of his loved one are black marks against his own critical judgment and against his initial estimate of the man. And so he takes pains to gloss them over and to keep the news quiet by loudly denying it. The result is a great monkey-show in which genuine talent is often made mock of by a persistent refusal to admit that it is never anything but topnotch.

§ 21

Don't hesitate to indulge in personalities. The common notion that there is something *infra dignitatem* about too personal criticism is just as silly as most other commonly held notions about criticism. When you are met with this personality blather, quietly refer your counsellor to such unseemly critical dealers in personalities as the Messrs. Cervantes, Voltaire and Zola or, if your counsellor has never heard of them, to Walkley, Archer and Shaw.

§ 22

Don't go too far with the idea that there are no rules in the case of drama. There happen, fortunately or unfortunately, to be a few. Bumptiously to deny the existence of all such rules is to make one's self out a ninny. There are certain rules. What there are not, are commandments.

§ 23

There is such a thing as a too great receptivity and liberal-mindedness on the part of a critic. The eagerness to miss nothing potentially worthy, to welcome talent in new fields and forms and to keep just a little ahead of the critical procession periodically leads the too open-armed critic into deplorable errors of judgment. Receptiveness and hospitality are valuable qualities in a critic, but they must be watched as closely as so many unleashed dogs, that they may not get out of hand, bark up the wrong trees and mess up things generally.

Many peculiar estimates have been confected by critics whose cordiality of attitude has for the moment got the better of their sense of sound discrimination. Need I point, for example, to George Moore, surely an otherwise even bitterly cautious critic, and his warm hugging of such playwrights as Léon Hennique, Oscar Méténier and Michael Field, to Edmund Gosse's blanket embrace of Strindberg as both dramatist and novelist, or to Huneker and his over-valuation of Maeterlinck, to say nothing of the half-dozen or more lesser and already forgotten geniuses whom he over-enthusiastically patted on the head?

§ 24

I am not so sure about the criticism we hear against special pleading. Is it always so ruinous to drama as they say it is? Is it too much to refer these critics, for example, to Shakespeare?

§ 25

You will be told never to sit down to write unless you have something to say beforehand. This is the veriest buncombe; pay no attention to it. Some of

16

the best things that a man writes occur to him after he has seated himself at his desk without the vaguest preliminary notion of what he was going to write—even, indeed, when he has cursed God for ever having put a pencil in his hand. Many a writer has produced something excellent after staring blankly at his pad of paper for hours. Ideas frequently come out of one's dull pencil in time as clear water comes eventually out of a muddy tap.

§ 26

A sound piece of criticism has never yet been spoiled by an injection of humor, let the professors yell all they want to. There is a place for apt humor in even the most serious work. If there is a place for it in "Hamlet," why shouldn't there be a place for it in a criticism of "Hamlet"?

§ 27

What constitutes a good play? There is no definition that meets the case, save it be some such completely obvious and broadly empty one as is now and then dispensed by the writers of dramatic text books. Any other attempt precisely to pigeon-hole

17

the problem must meet with failure, since the moment you think up an apparently sound and satisfactory definition along comes an artist who writes a good play that your definition fails to cover. Thus, the definition chefs, full of Aristotle's unities, were put to rout by Georg Kaiser. Thus, full of wisdom about dramatic action, they were set to chasing their tails by Sierra and Shaw. And thus, full of dramaturgic rules and regulations, they have been flouted by Strindberg, Wedekind, Schnitzler, Evreinoff, Synge, Dunsany, Gorki, Pirandello, Hasenclever and many others. A good play must have action? Then what of "Professor Bernhardi"? A good play must have love interest? Then what of "Pasteur"? A good play must be built around a single dominating character? Then what of "Night Refuge"? A good play must be fitted into the three-hour theatrical span? Then what of O'Neill's "Strange Interlude"? A good play must centre upon a conflict of wills? Then what of "The Cradle Song"? A good play must not mix its moods? Then what of "The Dream Play"? A good play must take its audience into its confidence

18

and not deceive it? Then what of "Seven Keys to Baldpate"? And so on, and so on.

The futility of any attempt to define exactly a good play may be illustrated no better, I daresay, than by giving a glance at the gymnastics of my alliterative colleague, Dr. Clayton Hamilton, author of "The Theory of the Theatre," "Studies in Stagecraft" and "Problems of the Playwright," "Any work of art is good," announces the professor, "if it forces the spectator or auditor to imagine and to realize some truth of life, and any effort of art is bad if it fails of this endeavor. Here is the final test of efficiency." What, one may relevantly inquire of the professor, is the particular truth of life that the auditor or spectator is forced to imagine and to realize by, let us say, Shaw's "Fanny's First Play," or D'Annunzio's "More Than Love," or Zoë Akins' "Papa," or Ibsen's "The Wild Duck"? Proceeding, the professor observes: "Any play, regardless of the method of the author, is a good play if it awakens the audience to a realization of some important aspect of the infinitely various assertions of the human will." To the realization of what important aspect of the infinitely various assertions of the human will, may I ask the professor, does Aristophanes' good play—and surely he will not deny that it is a pretty good play—called "Birds" awaken its audience? But yet the professor continues: "The good play must impose upon the spectator the educative illusion of reality; it must, by this means, increase vicariously his experience of life. It must lead the public out of living into life." Again, may one inquire politely of the professor how this phase of his definition manages to fit itself to, say, such a good play as "Chantecler," or "The Lady from the Sea," or "Ariane and Barbe Bleue," or "The Laughter of the Gods," or "Pippa Dances," or "The Dead City," or "The Hour Glass," or "Erdgeist," or "The Winter's Tale"?

COMEDY—POLITE AND OTHERWISE

§ 1

The designation, polite comedy, is a senseless one. There never was a so-called polite comedy worth a moment's consideration that was anything of the kind. The best of these polite comedies have, of course, possessed a veneer of manners, to say nothing of an impressive show of butlers, footmen, ladies' maids, tea carts, boutonnières, monocles and spats, but I can't at the moment recall one of them whose aforementioned gloss wasn't simply spread over a theme intrinsically as impolite as a gas bill collector. I shall not stupefy you with a catalogue of titles; you may readily appreciate the truth of the contention by trying to think of an exception. So-called polite comedy is merely vulgar comedy—I use the adjective in the best sense— made agreeable by a deft and worldly manipulation of the externals of the punctilio. If the characters insult one another after the manner of so many wop bus-boys, the playwright simply indicates that they must be dressed at their best when they go about the job and that their insults be couched in the epigrammatic form instead of in the lingo of shoot-'em-up melodrama. If the adultery committed by the characters is quite as vulgar and shoddy as that of the characters in cheap drama, the playwright further simply lays the scene in a room decorated in the Louis XV period instead of in one whose plaster is full of holes and the bed in which is offensively Grand Rapids. And if the actions of the characters, when closely looked into, are every bit as vulgar as those of the personages in the orthodox Broadway hokum, the writer merely covers up the fact by ridding them of the conventional dramatic indignations and loud voices and causing them to go about their vulgar doings with an air. Polite comedy, we thus find, is polite only as a servant is polite, that is, for business reasons. It is generically as dishonest in its politeness as a waiter expecting a sizeable tip. It has no intrinsic authenticity, no integrity as genuine polite comedy; it is merely vulgarity in fancy raiment as opposed

to drama, which is equally often vulgarity forthrightly naked. In the case of most polite comedies,
one gets the impression that the manners are the
result of personal insecurity on the part of the
authors and that the latter employ them to conceal
their ideational and dramatic nervousness as a
stockbroker at his first dinner in a hoped-for house
devotes himself exclusively—by way of safeguard-
ing himself from implemental *faux pas*—to the
salted nuts.

§ 2

The inability of American playwrights to brew
so-called polite social comedy out of the native
scene is less the fault of the playwrights, however,
than of the scene itself. Whenever one of these writers essays such a comedy, the howl of derisory
mirth when the curtain goes up can be heard a mile
away. He is informed, with a superior irony, that
society *grandes dames* are not in the habit of employing lorgnettes to survey the ashman, that gentlemen in Long Island country houses do not custom-
arily wear swallow-tails when they go to Canoe
Place to dance, and that it is hardly the fashion

at Bar Harbor to be uncomfortably elegant at breakfast. While it is true that the society plays visible on the American stage confuse the butler's pantry with the drawing-room and aristocracy with spinal paralysis, it is hardly less true that American society itself, in a number of its current manifestations, is guilty of a like confusion. One can't make bricks without straw, nor can one make plausible smart comedy where the basic materials are lacking.

The attempt at such comedy in America generally turns out to be ludicrous not because of the commonly voiced argument that its writers, not being of the class which they seek to depict, are unable to negotiate that depiction convincingly, but because the personages, life and pretensions with which they deal are in themselves essentially ludicrous. These are a subject for farce, not comedy. The fact that American actors are ill at ease in English drawing-room comedy is not strange; they are not to be blamed; it is not the circumstance that they are actors which brings about the embarrassment, it is rather the simple circumstance that they are Americans. A group of highly proficient actors drafted from American society, assuming that there were such a group, would be equally ill at ease. Before a nation may produce fashionable comedy it must produce a class to whom polish is not an acquired but a natural attribute. It must produce a class, first and foremost, so certain of its traditions and position that it can laugh at itself, for save it can laugh at itself it cannot persuade audiences to laugh with it. This laugh-with-it is the ground-plan of all effective polite comedy. In America, the situation is one of laugh-at-it, a situation, as I have observed, that makes only for open and shut farce. The fact that the majority of American writers who set themselves to polite comedy are alien to the polite world has nothing whatever to do with their failure. We have had a number of non-aliens to that world who have failed just as signally. The talented J. M. Patterson with his "Little Brother of the Rich" and Preston Gibson with his several comedies are examples that come to mind. Most of the best modern English drawing-room comedies, let us not forget, have been written by men who were far removed from the class which they described, by ex-traveling-salesmen, ex-actors, ex-shyster lawyers and ex-cattle-drivers, the sons, in turn, of farmers, provincial politicians, tradesmen and strolling players.

While the details of drawing-room comedy as it is manufactured by the unacquainted American playwright are sufficiently grotesque, the substance is often equally grotesque. For the details, such as causing the host and hostess at a Long Island week-end to call one of the housemaids into the party to do a Charleston—a toothsome morsel in one of the recent exhibits—, the ignorance of the playwright is alone to blame. But, ignorance or acquaintance, the playwright is less to blame for characters that are often in actual life unintentional caricatures. The so-called smartness of the best American polite comedy conceivable would immediately become transparently ridiculous were a character to stop suddenly short in his tracks in the middle of the play and ask each one of the other male characters to tell what his job was, and what his father's job was, in turn, before him. Truly smart drawing-room comedy presupposes the smartness of its characters; American drawing-room comedy builds up to it. There is a considerable difference between a Lord Quex and a former curb broker who has swindled enough money out of Florida real estate to rent a house at Newport.

§ 3

A scrutiny of the plays produced in New York in recent years reveals a uniform tendency on the part of native playwrights to fall into a fixed set of grooves in the manufacture of dialogic comedy. This comedy formula has been repeated for so long now that the edge has disappeared from it entirely. To be effective, comedy must have at least an air of spontaneity, and that which is currently being merchanted is as spontaneous as a railroad schedule. A regular theatregoer will immediately recognize it as following the appended half-dozen rubber-stamp forms:

1. *"What do you think you are? A——?"*

The attempt to extract laughter from this form takes the shape of exaggerated and ridiculous disparities. Thus does Mr. Perlmutter inquire ironically of Mr. Potash: "What do you think you are —a Valentino?", and thus, changing the form but slightly, does a host inquire sarcastically of a too ravenous eater: "What do you think this is—Reuben's?"

2. *"That isn't a——; that's a——!"*

The attempt to make the trade roll over in the instance of this one lies in the confection of impossible vaudeville antonyms. Thus, animadverting on avoirdupois, one character: "That isn't a stomach; that's Mount Logan!" And thus, objecting to the size of a tipple, another: "That isn't a drink; that's a tear!"

3. *"If that's a——, you're a——."*

Here the bait consists in hyperbolic contradictions. One character insists that what he is holding in his hand is a diamond. Whereupon, his *vis-à-vis:* "If that's a diamond, you're a grand piano." This is changed at times to the personality form, as "If you're a detective, I'm the Pope."

4. *"If I had a——like that, I'd——."*

This is the comic detraction form. "If I had a face like that," remarks a character, "I'd sue myself for damages." Or, "If I had a mind like that, I'd live in a sewer."

5. *"He's so——, he's——."*

No. 5 takes the shape of exaggerated disparagement. Alluding to B, A observes: "He's so mean he'd steal his own pants." Or: "He's so stingy, he makes his wife use old matches for toothpicks."

6. *"If——was——, I'd be——."*

The humor here proceeds from a character's chronic bad luck and his comment upon it, as "If it was raining money, I'd be wearing a mackintosh and galoshes," or "If diamonds was sauerkraut, my parents'd turn out to be French."

What we obviously have in these forms are a half-dozen branches on the family tree of the so-called wise-crack. The wise-crack is the species of repartee that from time immemorial has been accompanied on the vaudeville and burlesque stages either by a boot applied to its sponsor's seat or by a newspaper applied to his nose. It is humor that proceeds in no wise from character but simply from a dummy that serves as the mouthpiece of a ventriloquial stage writer. It relies for laughter solely upon itself; what has gone before it, whether in dialogue or character drawing or dramatic action or what not, is utterly immaterial. It may be isolated from its context and, unlike true comedic humor, lose nothing in the process. And it is today

29

the worst handicap under which American comedy writing is laboring. It has come to the stage directly from the movie sub-title and it has reduced dramatic composition on a wide-reaching plane to the level of such gag sub-titles.

The wise-crack, addressed theatrically to the cheaply vulgar element in our audiences, has not only already gone a long way toward ruining reputable comedy dialogue in the drama; it has already gone an even longer way toward ruining general conversation in the Republic. It is at present almost impossible to carry on an intelligent conversation with the average man or woman whom one meets. Before three sentences have passed, the snappy retort, the hypothetically jocose crack, the curbstone rejoinder, begin to show themselves. The nation is laboring under the belief that conversation is no longer conversation unless it be interlarded with a number of presumably devastating witticisms. Barbers filter Joe Miller through Bugs Baer; servant girls are jitney Mesdames de Staël; lawyers talk as if they were playing "in one"; Senators need only red undershirts and floppy pantaloons to get jobs with Mr. Albee. The young of the species, both male and female, talk like so many He and She jokes, and their elders like so many Harold Lloyd captions. The stage mirrors the taste of these idiots. There was a time when one man or woman in every ten thousand spoke at least the language of Bronson Howard's "Young Mrs. Winthrop." Today, the language is prevailingly that of Mr. Gleason's "Is Zat So?"

The bulk of the comedies on view in the American theatre at the present moment haven't characters, but merely interlocutors and end-men. Smear burnt cork over them and you'll find just so many minstrel shows.

§ 4

The difference between the approach to risqué sex comedy on the part of an American and a Frenchman is this: the American goes about the business with the air of one saying, "Isn't this interesting?" and the Frenchman with the air of one saying, "Isn't this ridiculous?" In these two points of view lies the secret of the Frenchman's ability to go the distance without offence and, on the contrary, the American's inability to do the same thing.

31

The French comedy writer gives one the effect of standing apart from his comedy and criticizing its naughtiness with a somewhat cynical indifference; the American gives one the impression that he is whole-heartedly playing the leading characters himself. And what is true of the American is also true of the German.

Although playwrights of other nations have often in more recent years tried to fashion risqué sex comedy in the tone and spirit of the French, they have seldom succeeded. A leer, however slight, has got into their work. They make one feel that, in a way, they have their eyes on their own heroines. One of the few exceptions that I can think of is Molnar's "Spiel im Schloss," which captures the boulevard quality nicely. What is this quality? It is not, as the American reviewer likes to describe it, an adroit skating over thin ice; it is, I believe, rather a complete and ingratiating lack of consciousness that there is any thin ice present to be skated over. If a playwright, whether because of nationality, race, geographical morals or what not, is unduly conscious of thin ice, his gingerly adjustment of his skates to it betrays him, and his written word no less. His very caution implies that he regards his theme as risky and even dirty, however much he may posture himself to the contrary. But where there is no self-consciousness over the matter of thin ice, the playwright's very unconcern throws the auditor pleasantly off the track. A child, knowing no taboos, may safely say things that, in the mouth of an older person, would call for the bouncer. It is this child-attitude in risqué sex writing that gives it the necessary innocence, and makes it theatrically safe. The Frenchmen, in their confection of such comedy, are figuratively little boys in long trousers.

It is the custom of the Anglo-Saxon theatrical commentator disparagingly to observe of the authors of such things as "Spiel im Schloss" that they do not take the theatre seriously. Nothing could be more foolish. They take the theatre seriously, but not the audience. The writing of good risqué comedy demands a serious craftsman, and one who understands the theatre down to the last inch. Is "The Wife Without a Smile" a less seriously considered piece of dramatic writing than "The Second Mrs. Tanqueray"? Is "L'Illusionniste" a less penetrating criticism of life and love than "Deburau"? Were the Restoration comedy writers mere empty clowns? Isn't "Les Hannetons" a much finer piece of work than "La Femme Seule" or "Maternité"? Which would an intelligent man rather see: "Reigen" or "Der Ruf des Lebens"? The commentators confuse themes with treatment. The dramatist who takes the theatre most seriously is often the one who picks his themes most lightly.

§ 5

A year or so ago, there was produced in New York an attempt at Restoration comedy by a Mr. Dorrance Davis called "A Lady in Love." The reviews of the effort read as if the author had been guilty of profaning the graves of the Twelve Apostles. It appeared that Davis had a high impudence to think that he had even a faint measure of Congreve's wit, that it was rank effrontery for him to set himself to capture the comic spirit of the Restoration period, and that he should at least have had the modesty to refrain from posturing himself in the position of the worthy dramatists who flourished in the time of the second Charles.

34

I hope that I do not unduly injure my colleagues'
feelings when I venture the opinion that though,
as they very rightly contended, Davis' attempt was,
to be generous, not especially successful, it was
still no worse and even a lot better than a number
of the comedies produced during the Restoration.

It seems to be a conviction of the gentlemen who
write about our theatre that the Restoration comedies were all extremely finished and very witty,
if, alas, sometimes bawdy, affairs. Say Restoration to them and their minds centre immediately
upon such exhibits as "The Way of the World,"
"Love for Love," "The Country Wife," "The
Double Dealer," and "The Beaux's Stratagem,"
much as if, fifty years from now, one were to
mention the Coolidge period in American drama
and the minds of their grandsons were to centre
solely upon the plays of Eugene O'Neill and
George Kelly. But the comedies of the Restoration,
unfortunately, were often quite as sorry specimens
in their way as many of the plays of the
Coolidge reign are in theirs. The Restoration had
its Davises, relatively speaking, as well as its
Wycherleys, just as the Coolidge period has had its

Mae Wests along with its Maxwell Andersons and Maurine Watkinses. If "A Lady in Love" had been written by a Davis of the Seventeenth or early Eighteenth Century, the present reviewers would undoubtedly have found merits in it that they currently decline to find. It is, as I have said, very, very far from a worthy comedy, but it is every bit as good, for example, as Aphra Behn's "The Forced Marriage," "The Debauchee" and "The Town Fop," Settle's "Fatal Love, or the Forced Inconstancy," Crowne's "The Country Wit" and "The Married Beau," or even Shadwell's "The Sullen Lovers." The wit and grace of the Restoration are too often taken for granted by those who have not gone to the pains (pains is the word) to read beyond its four outstanding figures, Congreve, Wycherley, Vanbrugh and Farquhar, or, possibly, to stretch a point, Etherege. Time has hallowed, in at least certain quarters, the excessive dulness of Buckingham and Rochester, beside whom the present-day Vincent Lawrence and even Harry Wagstaff Gribble are wits of the first water. Cibber, Otway and Sedley are prattled about in classrooms by professors who believe that anything with a cobweb on it is *ipso facto* more greatly worth consideration than something on which the paint is still wet and sticky, and who have not the faintest idea how inferior in every particular "The Careless Husband," "Friendship in Fashion" and "The Grumbler" are to any number of second-rate comedies shown every season on Broadway.

§ 6

One is brought to speculate on how much longer the epigrammatic form of expression will survive in the theatre. That the sounds of funeral bells are already in the air is unmistakable. However tasty an epigram may be in these days, it no longer gets the proper reaction from an audience. As a matter of fact, it doesn't take a close observer to note that an audience today has little use for the epigram and that this form of wit frankly bores it. The reason is a simple one. Through protracted usage, the humorous device that is the epigram has lost its theatrical availability, much as, through equally protracted usage, such bits of humorous stage business as the sudden gesture to the hip, indicating the drawing forth of a revolver and the pulling out instead of a handkerchief, have lost theirs. The vital element of surprise is no longer present. From long familiarity with the epigrammatic form, the audience knows, in a manner of speaking, just what to expect. What is more, there has come to be about the epigram a disturbing prefatory suggestion of the killing quip. When a character lifts his lips from a tea cup, nonchalantly adjusts his cravat and starts to open his mouth to negotiate a *jeu d'esprit*, the feeling is as if there were ever present a large placard lettered: "Now here's a tidy one!" The instant an epigram gets under way it betrays and defeats itself by the become-recognized humorous groove into which its wit is cast. The "Now I'm going to crack a good bit of repartee" air has it by the heels before it starts.

THE SABBATICAL THEATRE

I am frequently brought to task by certain otherwise edifying and sagacious critical professors
for an intermittent taste which takes me, with an
obvious and apparently lamentable relish, to the
lower forms of theatrical amusement. For this
taste, I am denounced as a trivial and flippant fellow, one to whom the grandeurs of Ibsen, Strindberg, *et al.*, must, for all his pretence to the contrary, remain esoteric and unappreciated. Surely,
runs the bull of excommunication, anyone who can
find enjoyment in burlesque shows, French farces,
hoofers, slapsticks and music hall skits in which a
gentleman with a deplorable hang-over gets into
bed with a Chinaman under the impression that
the Chinaman is Gaby Deslys, must be not only
something of an ass *per se*, but a customer anæs-
thetic to the good, the true and the beautiful in
dramatic art.

Of course, anyone who has practised criticism

professionally for a considerable space of time recognizes that such other critics are simply at the old trick of giving a public pundit-show, that they really know very much better, and that they themselves, in one way or another, are periodically guilty of equally low, and privately welcome, tastes. Take the late Walkley, for example, surely a cultivated and eminently estimable dramatic critic, if ever there was one. Two months before he passed to his Maker, one found him, immaculate in top hat and pince-nez, conducting himself thus professorially for the benefit of the conventions: "Plays of serious thought demand serious thinking about them. No adequate criticism is possible of, say, 'The Master Builder,' without equivalent brainwork. You can treat it superficially. You may say you prefer a Manhattan cocktail to it. You may declare it too frumpishly Scandinavian for your taste. But that is not criticism . . ." Having duly taken a bow at the applause, one then found him, in critical négligé, coming out exactly one month later with this somewhat confounding confession: "People flocked to Ibsen's plays (at the beginning) not for the fun of the thing, not to enjoy the art of drama, but as a solemn rite, to discern a 'message' . . . I also took service and slung much ink at the opposite party. My excuse is that I was young, or youngish. But I was never an Ibsenite and after 'The Master Builder' I broke away from the 'master' . . . 'What a crew!' you used to mutter to yourself as you came into an audience of Ibsenites gloating over Miss Elizabeth Robins' thick-soled boots and alpenstock as she bade her old architect mount his tower in 'The Master Builder' . . . Yes, and 'What a crew!' you were often tempted to say over the queer, uncouth, ill-bred people on the stage—the gentlemen who wore frock coats (of course, with pot-hats, they *would*) on the most inappropriate occasions, the touzled, disputatious women . . . the whole tagrag and bobtail . . ." And then,—after a few regulation academic pats on old Henrik's back—thus, by way of grand summing up and finale, the engagingly truthful Arthur Bingham: "But, to be frank, Ibsen is a little too grim, too hyperborean for my personal taste. Give me the *joie de vivre* and the Ziegfeld 'Follies' every time!"

The exclamation mark was Mr. Walkley's own.

But Walkley was not alone in his honesty. There are others who, in their off moments from the occasionally necessary professor-doctor show, similarly betray the intermittent depravity of their personal fancies. Shaw has frankly confessed that he gets a reprehensible amount of enjoyment out of Charlie Chaplin and Harold Lloyd moving pictures. The late William Archer told me confidentially one night over a mug of Bass that Florence Mills and her troupe of colored hoofers and slapstick smokes were, so far as he was concerned, a gift from the gods. Thomas Hardy, on the rare occasions he comes down to London, invariably picks out for the elevation of his psyche a music hall show wherein he can see one droll swat another across the beak with a London *Times*. The late James Huneker, as all his intimates knew, and as he on more than one occasion openly confessed in print, couldn't have been dragged to an Ibsen performance by a team of even brewery-wagon horses, where the mere news of a new pantaloon who chewed tobacco standing on his head and could shoot the wad with unerring aim into his watch-pocket was enough to make him call up his meri-

torious spouse instanter and inform her that he had
to stay in town that evening for a very important
conference with the Scribners. Georg Brandes had
a private penchant for the Danish equivalent of
"Why does a chicken cross the road?" and, up to
a few years before his death, was a secret patron
of any show that contained it. St. John Ervine, one
of the most talented of present-day English dramatic critics, who charmingly makes no bones
about what amuses him, has seen "Lady, Be Good"
almost as often as H. G. Wells. John Palmer's essay
on George Robey was one of the best things he ever
contributed to the *Saturday Review*. Alfred Kerr,
when he was over here, after the usual and necessary formalities, betook him to "The Cat and the
Canary" and enthusiastically reported that he
found *"die Spukregie meisterhaft,"* and then to the
colored show, "Shuffle Along," of which he freely
says in his book, "New York und London," *"Es
war mein stärkster Theater-abend in Amerika.
Fünfmal konnt' ich das hintereinander hören und
sehn!"*

"Great statesmen," says Schlegel, in his discussion of the part of the clowns in Shakespeare, "and

even ecclesiastics, did not consider it beneath their dignity to recruit and solace themselves after important business with the conversation of their fools; the celebrated Sir Thomas More had his fool painted along with himself by Holbein. . . . The dismissal of the fool has been extolled as a proof of refinement; and our honest forefathers have been pitied for taking delight in such a coarse and farcical amusement. For my part, I am rather disposed to believe that the practice was dropped from the difficulty in finding fools able to do full justice to their parts; on the other hand, reason, with all its conceit of itself, has become too timid to tolerate such bold irony; it is always careful lest the mantle of its gravity should be disturbed in any of its folds; and rather than allow a privileged place to folly beside itself, it has unconsciously assumed the part of the ridiculous; but, alas! a heavy and cheerless ridicule." "It may even be said that almost everywhere where there is happiness, there is found pleasure in nonsense," wrote Nietzsche. "Joy is timid," observed Anatole France, "and does not like festivals." . . . The mind, like the body, also needs its holidays. Imagine living in a world populated exclusively by profound philosophers. Imagine, in another direction, a world designed not by a fallible God, but by a relatively infallible Michelangelo, absolutely symmetrical, undeviatingly beautiful, without imperfection, intolerable. Imagine a world in which all the birds sang Bach, in which the sky was always like Monet's, in which the flowers knew no weeds, and in which human beings, all of them, moved with the eurythmic grace of Mordkins and Pavlowas. Imagine, in conclusion, a stage occupied everlastingly with the "Medea," "King Lear," "Little Eyolf," "The Father," "Gabriel Schilling's Flight" and "Herod."

The man of sound taste and of sound appreciation of fine art revels in an occasional departure from æsthetics and in a Gothic spree. Such an artistic sabbath serves the same purpose as do, in another direction, alcohol and tobacco. A Galsworthy and a Chesterton read detective stories when their higher tastes take their coats off and go on the loose, as a Richard Strauss slides down behind a *Seidel* and gives his ear to Broadway jazz. Mr. Paul Elmer More may deny convincingly that he can get the slightest amusement out of "Gentlemen

Prefer Blondes," but James Stephens, Dreiser, Hugh Walpole and Sherwood Anderson admit that they can get a lot. When Max Reinhardt landed here for the first time a few years ago, he sneaked away from his host, who insisted upon taking him to an art production of one sort or another, and went to the "Follies." Augustus John, while in America, was a regular customer of Minskys' Winter Garden, where no chorus girl weighs under two hundred pounds. Aldous Huxley, after a trip halfway 'round the world, made a bee line from the West Eighteenth street dock to "Cradle Snatchers." When Dunsany was last in America, I took him to a performance at the Plymouth of Gorki's "Nachtasyl," and he hasn't forgiven me yet. What he had wanted to see was the show down at the Olympic. Ernest Newman spent a half-dozen evenings in New York listening to George Gershwin's jazz. The late Percival Pollard's tribute to Herr Lautensack is known to perusers of his "Masks and Minstrels." Go back among the years. Hazlitt, in "Lectures on the English Comic Writers and Miscellaneous Essays," confesses his occasional excursions from sacrosanct taste in his delight over such an episode in "The Wonder" of Mrs. Centlivre as that wherein Don Felix, pretending to be drunk, forces his way out of Don Manuel's house by pretending that his marriage contract is a pocket-pistol, to the terror and confusion of the gentleman who would restrain him. "It," chuckles Hazlitt, "is one of the richest treats the stage affords!" Goethe's recourse to Sir Walter Scott and the peculiar belief that, because Scott amused him so in his off moments, Scott was therefore a great artist, is too well known to need rehearsal. And Richard Wagner listened with unfeigned pleasure to beer-garden tenors.

The hypocrisy of the professors in the matter of an occasional dose of good, juicy, low stuff and the sabbatical stimulation it provides to professorship of taste and judgment grown temporarily a bit weary of itself, is to be appreciated by a moment's glance at theatrical and dramatic chronology. Time has hallowed these very sabbatical stimulations of the past and thus made a nose at such critics as today deplore a taste for their modern counterparts. There is as much cheap, low, slapstick stuff in Aristophanes as there is in an Al Reeves' burlesque show, yet the bathos of distance has brought the professors to regard it as art. Shakespeare employed insanity to give his audiences some low burlesque chortles exactly as C. M. S. McLellan has done in "The Belle of New York," or as the Messrs. Dickey and Goddard have done in "The Misleading Lady," or as Sam Mann does in the vaudeville halls, and his crazy characters are to-day regarded by the professors as appropriate subjects for prolonged and serious clinical metaphysical study. Ibsen wrote "The Wild Duck" to give the more intelligent critics a laughing day off from what had come to be regarded as Ibsenism, and the idiotic professors of today go to it as if it were their best girls' funeral.

ACTORS AND ACTRESSES

§ 1

Just why it is that the average actor or actress cannot laugh in a way to make one believe for the moment that the laughter is genuine, I don't know. The average performer can cry in a perfectly convincing manner; he can express fear, hate, alarm and most of the other emotions with a very fair degree of realism. But when it comes to opening his mouth and shaking his midriff he is about as successful in conveying illusion as a stage horse-race. Perhaps it is because, of all the emotions, high merriment is the most difficult of expression save one actually and deeply experience it within one. Joy is an ever mysterious thing, since it is experienced by the human being but seldom, where disappointment and its attendant dejection are experienced almost daily. The actor, after all, is a human being like many of the rest of us, and he apparently cannot counterfeit an emotion of which he actually knows so little and which is strange to him. The other emotions he has had a comparatively intimate acquaintance with, and so they offer him much less resistance. But laughter, deep, rib-shaking laughter, baffles him. He is able to imitate its sound, but he is unable to get beneath the surface-sound and push it up from below with his heart.

Consider the manner in which, when their rôles demand, certain of our more conspicuous actors and actresses perform the business of loud laughter. Mr. Otis Skinner's has the sound of a thumb and forefinger being run along a resined cord attached to an old baking-power can. Mr. John Barrymore's has the sound of an arpeggio executed on a xylophone that has been left out in the rain. Mr. Holbrook Blinn laughs like water running out of a bath-tub, and Mr. Louis Mann like a piccolo muffled with a dishrag. Miss Rambeau, when she seeks to express loud mirth, sounds much like a fish fork struck against an umbrella jardinière, and Miss Lynn Fontanne like someone falling upon a banjo. Nor are their brothers and sisters much happier.

§ 2

One of Mrs. Fiske's latest contributions to the art of acting is a performance of "Ghosts" that emphasizes what strike the lady as being the underlying humorous aspects of the drama. Her performance has, of course, been hailed as a new interpretation, which—like playing Bach on a saw —it assuredly is, and as a remarkable example of intellectual exercise, which—like penciling a moustache on the Venus de Milo—it perhaps is not. The critical reception of any such histrionic shenanigan as this of Mrs. Fiske's is always accurately to be anticipated. A so-called new interpretation of any classic, however idiotic, usually persuades the commentators to a veneration of its impresario's cerebral gifts, when all that is actually discernible is an actor's sly effort to conceal his histrionic deficiencies, readily detectable from familiarity with past excellent interpretations of the rôle, by artfully giving a wholly different version of the rôle and thus temporarily throwing the critics off their guard and getting rid at one swoop of all derogatory comparisons.

This new interpretation balderdash has become a pet chicane on the part of producers who hate the idea of paying royalties, craftily lay hold of one of the classics and hope to put it over on the jays as something relatively new and lively by arbitrarily doing it in a way—preferably senseless—with which the aforesaid jays are not familiar. And no less a favorite dodge has it become of actors and actresses who desire to achieve a bit of facile *kudos* by passing themselves off as sterling intellects on the ground that they are able to see something in a classic that no one else has ever seen in it, including the author, and that is not there. All that an actor or actress who hasn't had a job for five years need do today to get him or herself viewed as a somebody is to hire a theatre and play Juliet as an Owen Davis ingénue in a Lanvin frock or Hamlet as a character out of William Gillette's "Held by the Enemy." Mrs. Fiske has simply resorted to what should be a perfectly transparent monkeyshine and, say what you will against her, has succeeded in getting exactly the reaction that she had in mind. Her Mrs. Alving is no more Ibsen's—and if she is in any honest personal doubt on the score, one need only refer her to the dramatist's notes—than it is Mr. Samuel Shipman's.

It is, of course, possible to read humor into portions of any tragedy, and in such a way, if the performer be a clever one, that the less tutored among the critics will be persuaded that it is justified by the text. As I once pointed out, all that one would have to do to convert "Little Eyolf," for example, into a very funny farce would be to play it word for word as written, but to have the actors chew gum. In the same way, and more seriously, even a casual reading of "Rosmersholm" or "John Gabriel Borkman" will betray numerous instances where a humorous reading is possible, if fundamentally absurd. Almost any classical tragedy offers loopholes for the species of dolts who like to laugh at funerals. And what is more, as I have already observed, with a measure of superficial justification. Humor may thus, with a fair degree of bobtail plausibility, be veined through the tragic loveliness of "Romeo" as through the woe and ache of "Lear." But it no more belongs there than it belongs in the Book of Ruth, although Mrs. Fiske, if she so desires, may as readily get it into the latter simply by emphasizing two little points that never were meant to be emphasized. Take, for example, some such passage out of tragedy as Hecate's speech on the heath or Othello's in the castle bed-chamber or, and this most surely, Cleopatra's in the palace at Alexandria. Certainly there is a possible humor, too, in these—if the author had only meant it to be humor. But the author plainly didn't mean it to be, and his text plainly doesn't mean it to be. And so with "Ghosts." We accordingly find Mrs. Fiske's performance to be of a piece with a vaudeville comedian's recitation of "The Raven."

§ 3

A series of visits to the Chinese theatre on the Bowery induces in one an amused contemplation of the commonly held notion that Chinese actors must be very remarkable fowl, indeed, to be able to master the repertoire of 365 or more different plays that their theatre annually calls upon them to appear in. For years, jerkwater college oracles have been returning from brief Cook's Tours to the Orient and writing learned treatises shaming the

Anglo-Saxon actor with accounts of the extraordinary virtuosity and versatility of the Chinese actor. So long has this nonsense been going on that most Americans have come to accept it as a serious fact. The average American who is at all interested in the theatre and drama of the world today believes that the Chinese stage is full of veritable Salvinis crossed with Zanzigs, great artists of histrionism with the memories of super-vaudeville mystics, performers who not only can memorize a different drama every day but who, to boot, can act it with a mighty and amazing talent.

It is true that a Chinese actor is called upon and is able to memorize several hundred more plays in a single season than the Anglo-Saxon or Latin actor, but anyone reasonably familiar with three-quarters of the kind of plays that one gets in the Chinese theatres will fail unduly to marvel at the fact. These plays are the veriest A, B, C; the most of them are fundamentally of a piece; they differ but slightly. Certain lines and much of the business are common to all of them. They impose little more strain upon the player's memory, provided he be a fellow of moderate experience, than

a single Anglo-Saxon play like "Abie's Irish Rose."
And they do not, from first to last, impose one-
fiftieth the strain that such a play as "Hamlet" or
"Chantecler" imposes. In addition, almost all the
Chinese plays that are presently acted in the Oriental theatres may be acted in exactly the same
way. The Chinese actor substitutes an elaborate
make-up for characterization; there is small need
for him to practise the details of physical movement, since there is a minimum of such movement called for; the necessary gestures are the
same in Play No. 1 as in Play No. 365; the need
for direction is utterly negligible. Even the speaking voice need not be closely watched, as all shadings are lost in the terrific noise that is manufactured during the progress of the plays by the Chinese racket-chefs seated to the right of the actors.

The buncombe has been spread among Occi-
dental students of the Oriental drama by critics
who, knowing absolutely nothing of the Chinese
language, have imagined that what the Chinese
actors were reciting must be very fine poetic stuff.
I am reliably informed by several cultured Chinese of my acquaintance that it is, in the main,

just about as fine and poetic as "It Was Christmas in the Harem" or "Yes, We Have No Bananas."

§ 4

The reason for the eminence in the French theatre of Madame Cecile Sorel is perhaps to be found in the woman rather than in the actress. Much as with the English, though to a lesser degree, are the French given to a devotion to actresses not so much for their public talent as actresses as for their private attractiveness as women. It is thus that favorites are conceived and bred, and once such a favorite is lodged in her niche nothing can remove her from it. The modern history of the English stage and that of the French is replete with the names of ladies who have been admired and eulogized over a long period of time for purely sentimental reasons. These, gifted with the power of adorning a stage without vitalizing it, have managed to confound their critics into believing that what is charming is also necessarily histrionic, and out of the confusion of values has flowered gradually the artificial bloom of their reputations.

Madame Sorel, I allow myself to believe, has profited magnificently by this critical delusion. Ask the average Frenchman what he thinks of her and you will find him admiringly replying, with unconscious significance: *"Hélas!* What a woman!" Not "What an actress!", note; but "What a woman!" And if there was ever an average Frenchman, I nominate as a type any one of the dramatic critics currently practising their art in France, with perhaps the single exception of the clear-sighted Henri Béraud. The Frenchman, in the case of Madame Sorel, as in the instance of a half-dozen of her less well-known contemporaries, sees the actress in terms of what she is, or impresses him as being, off the stage. He sees the actress primarily not in her costume and grease-paint and not in her stage rôles, but in her salon, her motor car, her worldly life. If that life massages his fancy with agreeable unguents, if about her there linger a tale and a tradition that gratify his imagination, he takes with him into his orchestra chair an already established idea and appraisal of her, and whatever the quality of her art that idea and that appraisal remain uppermost and dominant. The woman who thus strikes his fancy may be any one of a dozen kinds. She may be a creature of the gala world or she may be a home-body with two or three flaxen-haired children, the latter, particularly, if she be on the English stage. She may be the darling of princes, or the rage of Deauville and Monte Carlo, or the wife of a playwright-critic who is a member of a reciprocal back-patting fraternity. She may be a gracious and handsome woman with a gift for sweetening her five o'clock tea with sugary glances, or she may be one who with her own hands bandaged soldiers' wounds during the war and supported twenty or thirty war orphans. She may be any one of these, or something else, and a mediocre actress. But when she sweeps through the stage-door, she carries with her the external impression of her and whether she be a Camille or a Phèdre or a Paula Tanqueray to make the very ushers gnash their teeth, she remains still in the public estimation an admired and much loved creature.

While the precise ground whence has sprung the French admiration of Madame Sorel is unknown to me, it is certain that that admiration must be founded upon other things than her histrionic virtuosity. That she knows the rudiments of her trade, that she is mistress of the many tricks of acting and that she has even now and again, as in "Sans Gêne," given more than a merely creditable account of herself, are not to be denied. But that she comes anywhere near being the first-rate actress that her countrymen have persuaded themselves to imagine she is is a matter for very considerable doubt. I have seen Sorel, I believe, in almost every rôle of her repertoire in the last fifteen years and more, and I have yet to see a single dramatic performance of hers that could be fairly put down as anything better than second-rate. In comedy, she presents a more likely talent, as I have noted, than in drama. But in neither does she present a talent that glows and glistens and that reaches out over the footlights with an entire conviction. At her best, she is artificial; one can detect clearly the turning of the histrionic wheels; one can feel always the heavily conscious performer. The heat of fine acting may conceivably be in her mind, but she is unable to coax it down into her heart.

If I have seemed to imply that only in France

and England are favorites established in the manner I have intimated, I wish to correct the impression. For here in America we have occasionally engaged the same phenomenon. Maude Adams was an example. But the American goes in for that sort of thing very, very much less than the European and, what is more, he shows sign of abandoning it altogether. I know of no actress in the American theatre today who can give a series of second-rate performances and yet by the love of the public for her bring long lines to the box-office window. In France and in England, on the other hand, one would have small difficulty in naming names.

§ 5

About a year ago, Mrs. Patrick Campbell, after an absence of some fourteen years, made her reappearance on the New York stage at the Mansfield Theatre in a comedy called "The Adventurous Age." In the third act of the piece, the action called for Mrs. Campbell to crawl down a short ladder from the window of a house. Upon her negotiation of the feat, not without considerable

61

visible effort and audible puffing, a great wave of applause broke over the auditorium. Though plainly unintentional, that applause was so ironically insulting that it would not have surprised me in the least had Mrs. Campbell, were she not the well-bred woman she is, thereupon stepped to the footlights and in very polite terms bidden her audience to go to Hell.

The pathos and the significance of the incident should not be lost upon us. Here was an actress who in her heyday was a celebrated beauty; here was a woman who, aside from what acting talent she possessed, was once a slim and sightly creature to stimulate men's fancy, to turn the heads of countless cavaliers, to make tom-toms of innumerable masculine hearts, aye, even to cause the very dogs in Hyde Park to chase their tails with an unwonted pruritus. And what had time wrought of her? A Brünnhilde creased with the years, an old woman plainly strapped in to the point of discomfort, whose mere climbing down a few rungs of a little ladder without collapsing created a gaping astonishment in her audience. That way lay the pathos. And this way lies the significance: that no woman such as Mrs. Patrick Campbell was should, when the decades have stolen her physical splendors, risk longer the kindly derisions of an ever essentially cruel theatre.

There is nothing more sad and nothing more ridiculous than the spectacle of an ex-beauty fighting it out on the old line. The greatest actress in the English-speaking theatre of today is the *memory* of Mary Anderson; the most pitiable, the quondam proud beauty, whatever her name, who valiantly and idiotically and very tragically tries to make the memory of yesterday still walk alive in skirts and grease-paint. With certain actresses, of course, the case is different. For there are actresses far gone in years who never capitalized youth or beauty as their chief theatrical assets, who were made to seem relatively venerable in youth by the classics, who have devoted their careers to capturing the esteem of men who have drunk out of Shakespeare rather than out of silken slippers. These are the ageless actresses, for they never made a weapon of mere years, and they are thought of primarily as actresses and not as women. The history of the theatre is not without many such names. But there are others of whom the public has been made to think first as women and secondly as actresses, and by the women themselves. These have been those who have enveloped themselves in their younger years with a surface romance of one kind or another, and with plays that emphasized the romantic aspect of them. These are the women who have made capital of their physical charms and who have presented themselves to audiences over a long period as sirens of Lake Como week-ends, vampires of the Nile and the despair of young clergymen on their way to the Holy Land. It is these upon whom time plays its foulest tricks. It is these who, grown chunky and wrinkled and rubber-girdled, dare the mordant appraisal of audiences when vanity sacrifices them to the sharp steel teeth of its inevitable and merciless bear-trap. Mrs. Patrick Campbell is still a skilful comédienne, but what chance does mere skill at trivial comedy stand against the recollection of a once lovely woman become sere and fat and yellow?

§ 6

Whatever the poverty of the American theatre in other directions, it finds its cornucopia sufficiently full of talented clowns. I doubt that the theatre of any other country at the present time can boast so many genuinely droll fellows, or that when it comes to low comedy there is a factory so productive of salubrious guffaws. On what country's stage will you discover another Bobby Clark with his stogie butt, elegant walking stick and illuminated diamond; Harpo Marx dragging a long rope after him, disappearing in the wings and presently reappearing at the other side of the stage holding its still trailing end; and Tom Healy trying vainly and with much grave head-scratching to figure out how his partner guesses what number he has been thinking of, when the former asks him and he tells him and his partner says "That's correct"? Or George Bickel with such a German dialect as hasn't been heard in the American air since Jim Huneker used loudly and with much banging on the table to order biscuit Tortoni at Lüchow's; Phil Baker ironically inquiring of Sid

65

Silvers if he knows what pinochle is and Silvers replying, "Sure! Pinochle and sauerkraut"; and W. C. Fields and his majestic, cuff-shooting mien, modish dickey and very tony cigar end? Or Al Jolson swapping confidential matters with a horse; Eddie Cantor bounding back and forth across the stage, the while he with a consuming enthusiasm relates the astounding wonders of being bitten lovingly on the ear by a red-headed girl; and Bert Wheeler singing a tearful ballad the while he eats a large cheese sandwich and dill pickle? Or Poodles Hanneford with his rubber suspenders that, when he would adjust them to his pantaloons, elude his grasp, shoot back and clap him a jolly one in the eye; Sam Mann and his lemon lozenge sucked tormentingly near the orchestra brasses; and Will Mahoney and his derby? Or Moran and Mack; Eddie Conrad and his piano act; and Frank McIntyre with his two-ton lizzie walk? Or Tom Patricola's clown clogging; Will Rogers' animadversions on politics; Julius Tannen's monologues; and Walter Catlett's priapic love-making? Or Joe Cook's reading of a bedtime story; the unmatched paint-smearing act of the Ardath brothers; Andrew Toombes' fairy tale; McIntyre and Heath's travelogue on ham trees, pretzel vines and pork-chop bushes; and Raymond Hitchcock's chronic case of laryngitis? Or Victor Moore's baby voice; Fred Stone with his serio-comic athletic monkey-shines; Lew Fields with his shoulder-shrugging, philosophical "Easy come, easy go" upon being swindled out of the one hundred dollars that represent his life's savings; and Don Barclay and Al Herman? Or Bozo Snyder and Sliding Billy Watson of the burlesque houses; Tom Howard and his dopey "Spy" act; and Frank Tinney, on such occasions as he is out of the hospital, with his orchestra leader conversazione? Or Joe Smith, of the Avon Comedy Four, and Ted Lewis, and, surely, Johnny Hudgins and his hoofing panto-mime, and Joe Jackson and his bicycle, and the excellent Ed Wynn, and Harry Watson and his prize-fighter act, and Gallagher and Shean, and Jack Donahue, and Herb Williams and his piano act, and Gus Shy, and Chick Sale? These occur to my pencil as it travels quickly across paper. There are others, I am certain, that I have over-looked—others who rank with many of these as professors of the belly-laugh. In combination, they comprise a company the like of which only the American House of Representatives can equal.

§ 7

Contemplating the performances of Raquel Meller once again, one is brought to the renewed conviction that the great success of the lady in working her spell over an audience is due hardly at all to what she does but rather almost entirely to what she is. There are many performers who can sing a hundred times better than she can, who can step the few steps that she steps with a doubled suavity of foot and who are more expert in gesture, in eye-rolling and in physical grace, but I know of none who is so utterly permeating a *woman*. Raquel Meller is the triumph of a remarkably powerful theatrical personality over her art. That art amounts to very little, but the woman that is La Meller amounts to the most persuasive female on view to us in this day.

I hesitate to ascribe Meller's enormous power over an audience to sex, since that is often the easiest way out of describing anything that baffles one. But that is nevertheless just what it is. If I am mistaken, I shall be glad to publish a retraction as soon as someone comes forward with a better and more convincing explanation. Meller is a complete dramatization of sex. Her every look, every movement, every intonation are full of it. She is not young; she certainly is not beautiful; but she is like sleepy electricity. She creeps over the footlights like an odorless incense, hypnotically, alluringly. She is like a convent on fire.

Yvette Guilbert intellectualized her songs; Meller simply suggests the emotion that they produce in her. More, she suggests that emotion in its mildest possible theatrical terms. She sings a lyric as Clare Kummer would write it. She never obtrudes an emotion for a moment; there it is, she seems to say, and what about it? She never hints dramatically that anything is important; she is casual and indifferent toward her material; she sings, as it were, through half-closed eyes. Her audience is a matter of seeming unconcern to her and she gets it into the hollow of her hand for that very reason.

I have read that Meller is a great actress. She is. But not exactly in the way the tribute has been intended. She is a great actress not as certain other women are great actresses; she is a great actress in that she can move and hold audiences by sheer negative acting. She is not a positive, histrionically speaking; she is a negative. Her art is a denial of acting and a theatrical affirmation of woman as woman. It is not Raquel Meller who acts; it is Raquel Meller who makes her audiences act, as a magnet makes steel tremble and move.

Nothing could conceivably be more banal than the material the tonadillera selects with which deliberately to merchant her sex. "El Relicario," for example, is the ancient lyric which tells of the bull-fighter who, dying, presses to his lips the memento of his lady-love. "Diguili Que Vengui" tells of the coy maiden who, reconsidering the proposal of her lover, sends him a message to return to her waiting arms. "El Peligro de las Rosas" is our old friend about the thorn that lurks in every rose. "Noi de la Mare" is the one about the bereft mother at her dead baby's cradle. "Ay! Cipriano" is a Spanish version of the famous "Bump Polka" song made familiar to us fifteen years ago in "The

Queen of the Moulin Rouge." "La Hija del Carcelero" is the hokum about "the only prison I wish for thee is the prison of my heart." "La Tarde del Corpus" is about the girl who is betrayed and who pulls a stiletto out of her sock and stabs her deceiver. "La Monteria" is the bewhiskered lyric about "grandma's day." "Flor del Mal" is sentimental whangdoodle about "a poor little flower of sin." "Mimosa" is the one about the heartless coquette. "Gitanelle" is the one about "my gipsy sweetheart." "La Violetera," you know. "Siempre Flor" goes on about the life of a woman being even as the life of a flower. In "Nena," a dying lover repeats his promise of eternal fidelity, as if the poor nut could henceforth be anything other than biologically faithful. And "La Farandula Pasa" is our venerable camarado, the one about Pierrot who "sows gladness where there has been only sadness."

Over such stuff, the international aphrodisiac that is Raquel Meller triumphs. Let the boys stop this nonsense about her great histrionic virtuosity and tell the truth.

§ 8

"He believes that he has discovered a new instinct, hidden from psychologists until this year of grace—the instinct of transformation, or the instinct of theatricalization." Thus, one of the literary critics in a summation of the latest philosophical crumb of the Russian Evreinoff. That our Slav friend has actually discovered something new, however, is to believed only by those who are unaware of John Palmer's distillations from the elaboration by Wilde of Shakespeare's meditations upon the same subject. Taking the latter's familiar "All the world's a stage," Wilde pursued the truth further in his equally familiar treatise on nature's invariable imitation of art. And taking Wilde's animadversions as a spring-board, Palmer splashed around amusingly in the theory that so great was life's imitation of the drama that today when a man found his wife had been unfaithful to him he generally met the situation with a line out of a Pinero play. All that Evreinoff has done is to expand Palmer's idea, originally set forth brilliantly in an essay in the *Saturday Re-*

view, into a book. And as a book, whatever its shortcomings, always makes much more impression than an essay—in the same way that a skyscraper always makes much more impression than a smaller building, however superior architecturally the latter—we find Evreinoff hailed as a profound fellow the while Palmer is brushed aside.

The impulse toward theatricalization has long been as habitual to human beings as their impulse to lie to themselves in most other directions. It begins in childhood with boys playing the rôles of Indians, firemen and policemen, and with little girls "playing house" and mothering doll babies; it continues into adolescence with an imitation in dress and deportment of objects of their admiration; it goes on into the twenties with boys patterning their conduct after celebrated football heroes and movie actors, and girls patterning theirs, in turn, after the heroines of romance; it grows, rather than diminishes, with age's coming and finds men and women offering to the world spurious and somewhat idealized projections of themselves, that the world may be persuaded to accept them for what they actually are not. It is thus that we have the Napoleon complex in countless business men, the Valentino complex in innumerable fake cavaliers, the Nietzsche complex in various jitney radicals, the Tunney complex in weaklings—after they have swallowed a couple of cocktails—, and the Cleopatra face-powder and lip-rouge of shopgirls, together with Turkish incense attempting to lend an Oriental air to Harlem flats, clerks dressing themselves up to look like an approximation to the Prince of Wales, bowlegged and knockkneed women trying to shortskirt themselves into the wallop of a Peggy Joyce, and thousands of Fords equipping themselves with twenty-five-dollar foghorns and hoping to convince startled pedestrians that they are Hispano-Suizas.

The tremendous jump in the trade of interior decoration, with its penchant for converting bedrooms of the Benjamin Harrison period into Du Barry boudoirs and Grand Rapids sitting-rooms into George Alexander drawing-rooms, marks simply the growing tendency to bring the stage into the American home. So, too, does the increase in the use of soft lamps, and the increase of English servants, and the increase in triangular emotional sport. In the way of individuals, it was at times almost impossible to distinguish William Jennings Bryan from Robert B. Mantell, just as it is at times difficult to distinguish between the Hon. Mr. Dawes and a dress rehearsal of "What Price Glory?" A Mrs. Snyder plays the rôle of a Paul Armstrong heroine; a Governor of the State of New York acts the rôle of a Paul Bourget hero; a hundred thousand little stenographers droop their mouths like Dolores Costello and drive their bosses to drink making Mae Murray bed-room eyes. Small wonder that theatrical and moving picture censorship is a grim necessity.

§ 9

Gentleman of the old school though I am, and ever ready to defend the ladies with my chivalrous Virginia blood, I am yet constrained to protest against the current custom of casting the leading rôles in musical comedy with ladies apparently so advanced in years. Against ladies of advanced years, I have, in general, nothing; but when producers cast one of the otherwise estimable creatures for the breath-taking, beautiful and excessively phallephoric princess in musical shows, I fear that I forget myself. Age may at times be all very well for drama, but musical comedy calls for youth—and at the top of its lungs. There is a place for the old girls in drama, but, when the band strikes up, all genuinely serious critics and dyed-in-the-wool æsthetes demand something under thirty—both in the matter of years and calf circumference.

§ 10

There is a belief, still fondly nursed by certain critics, that if an actor be talented enough he can play almost any part, even one to which he may not physically be suited, and by the sheer exercise of his skill make his audience unconscious of his corporeal unfitness for the rôle. To this belief, I have devoted well nigh a quarter of a century to win myself, but with, I regret to have to report, a very dubious success. I hope I do not boast unduly when I say that I have perhaps as flexible an imagination as the next man. I am, indeed, at least so far as the theatre is concerned, able to hocus-pocus myself into imagining things that would make any competent alienist who happened to be a stranger to the theatre scratch his nose and shake his head meaningly. But this amazing imagination of mine rebels when it comes to grips with the problem of persuading myself that a fifty-year-old actor with a bald head and a sizeable belly becomes Little Lord Fauntleroy by the simple device of putting on velvet knee-pants and a blond wig, and by bringing to his interpretation a rich and varied experience in "The Lyons Mail," "Rosmersholm" and "The Marble Heart."

Do I exaggerate? A bit, no doubt, but not so much as some may believe. For every season reveals casting almost as ridiculous. Who fails to remember, for example, Mrs. Fiske's attempt to play a sixteen-year-old girl in the first portion of Edward Sheldon's "The High Road," or Nance O'Neil's recent effort to convince the trade, in the play called "Fog-Bound," that she was a wild young thing of seventeen or eighteen? And who does not recall Frank Gillmore in a yellow toupé trying to palm himself off as the youthful Karl in the New Theatre's production of "Old Heidelberg," Otis Skinner as the fiery bull-fighter in "Blood and Sand," Robert Edeson as the college boy in "Classmates," Madame Nazimova as the incalescent flapper in "Dagmar," Jacob Ben-Ami as the American husband in "Welded," or the papa who was cast for the little lad in the memorable production of Wedekind's "Awakening of Spring" a number of years ago at the Maxine Elliott Theatre? To cozen the imagination to accept such jocosities seriously is a job either for lay idiots or for professional critics given to a lingering schoolboy adulation of actors and to a comprehensive faith in that most bogus of mummer monkeyshines, versatility. Although an actor may in his day play many parts, he is generally found to play those parts best for which he is physically and temperamentally most patly suited. Mansfield, when he tried Prince Karl, made a spectacle of himself; Bernhardt did the same when she tried Joan; Maude Adams was ridiculous when she essayed the rôle of the cocky rooster in "Chantecler"; Ethel Barrymore's attempt at Juliet need not be recalled to you. Talent has nothing, or at best very little, to do with it; all the talent in the world can't duel successfully with Nature. Yet the actor is vain enough to try to remake God.

Life itself can tolerate no such casting as the drama often suffers. Mussolini must look his rôle to gain the favor of the world. The trouble with the Russian Bolshevists is that their leaders look too much like Trotsky and Lenin.

COPROPHILIA

§ 1

The professional moralist betrays himself by the very nature of his profession. Bereft of it, he would be as uncomfortable as a pig in a pew. He is what he is because filth, real or imaginary, gratifies him, albeit at times indirectly. You will never find a sewer repairer who can't stand the smell of sewage.

§ 2

It has become a platitude that when the moralist mind presently scans the drama its attention becomes fixed almost exclusively upon sex. With the death of Anthony Comstock there passed out of moral snooping, in all its departments and ramifications, the consideration of all other offences against the established hand-me-downs of Moses. Sex and sex alone became the turpentine that made the smut-smellers squirm and heave. To the late lamented Anthony, sex was but one evil calling for the intervention of the Lord God Almighty and Police Captain Mulcahy. There was, too, a comprehensive catalogue of other instruments of Satan. There were, as we discover after a study of the eminent Anthony's tome, "Traps for the Young," candy stores that retarded the footsteps of youngsters on their way to school and church, stories of romantic love, newspapers that printed accounts of crimes, dime-novels recounting the exploits of train robbers, safe-crackers, detectives and other such crooks, novels containing oaths, tales of gambling, pool-rooms, raffles, lotteries, plays dealing with criminals, alcoholic drinks, patent medicines, dubious professors of the *spirochaeta pallida*, booklets setting forth the ways and means of dropped-handkerchief and like flirtations, atheistic and infidel literature, and a score of similar corruptions.

Sex, indeed, was one of the least of the nefarious nuisances against which the august crusader pitched his indignations. In literature and in the drama, Comstock found many more things to deplore and prosecute than the mere over-active libido. Among the infamies that aroused his wrath and sent him hot-foot to the telephone to summon to his and Jehovah's aid the minions of the law were—I quote from his book—"coarse, slangy stories in the dialect of the bar-room, the blood-and-thunder romance of border life, and the exaggerated details of crimes, real and imaginary; crimes which are gilded and lawlessness which is painted to resemble valor, making a bid for bandits, brigands, murderers, thieves and criminals in general; leading characters who possess extraordinary beauty of countenance, most superb clothing, abundant wealth, the strength of a giant, the agility of a squirrel, the cunning of a fox . . . and who are the high favorites of some rich person who by his patronage and endorsement lifts the young villains into lofty positions in society and provides liberally of his wealth to secure them immunity for their crimes"; plays and stories in which "one girl is hired to personate a rich girl and marry the villain in her stead," in which "a beautiful girl, by lying and deceit, seeks to captivate one whom she loves," in which "a man is murdered by being blown up by explosives," in

which "assaults are made upon an officer while re-
sisting arrests," in which there is a "conspiracy
against an officer to prevent the arrest of a crimi-
nal," in which there is a "burglary or a woman
murdered by masked thieves," in which "an attempt is made to force a beautiful girl to marry a
scoundrel to save her benefactor," in which "attempts are made to coerce a girl to marry against
her wishes," in which there are attempted assassin-
ations, in which confidence games are shown or described, in which highwaymen figure, in which there
is a massacre by Indians, in which "one babe is
stolen to substitute for another," in which there is
clandestine correspondence between two sweet-
hearts, in which a man deserts his first wife and
marries another woman, in which there is "a disparagement of honest toil," in which such things
are shown, as "in what part of the body to plant
pistol bullets to the best advantage and how to handle poison skilfully," and in which "there are de-
falcations and embezzlements." Fifteen or twenty
additional items of like character are listed. Under the terms of them, Comstock advocated sup-
pression, and not on sex grounds, of all such theatri-

cal exhibits as "Is Zat So?", the melodramas of Lincoln J. Carter, "Within the Law," "Raffles," "Robin Hood," "The Bohemian Girl," "Pinafore," "The Prisoner of Zenda," "Night Refuge," "The Weavers," "The Fatal Card," "Sherlock Holmes," "Get-Rich-Quick Wallingford," "Turn to the Right," "Strife" and a hundred others currently regarded by his descendants in morality as innocent and harmless.

The moral order has turned something of a cartwheel since Comstock became a subject of interest for the worms. Where the moralist of the '80's saw harm in the depiction of countless human frailties and diversions, his offspring today sees danger *pur et simple* in sex. The drama may safely violate all the Commandments but the Seventh. Even the second clause of the Tenth is perfectly safe in any number of dramatic directions, as we know, for example, from plays, their placid courses left undisturbed, like "Pélléas and Mélisande," "Candida," "The Fugitive," "The Joy of Living," "Lady Windermere's Fan," "The Liars," "The Duel," "The Galilean's Victory" and "The Case of Rebellious Susan." But with the Seventh it is different.

And not only with that one literally, but with any and all approaches to it. One may speculate as to the reason. That reason, I believe, may be discovered in the fact, well appreciated by the blue-noses, that sex is the easiest foundation on which to erect the structure of a moral show to which the public will respond. The blue-noses seek self-advertisement above everything else; when Sumner in an unguarded moment foolishly agreed with the District Attorney's office to make his raids without publicity he spelled not only his own doom but the doom of financial contributions to his anti-vice society, as one of his latest pamphlets calling desperately for funds demonstrates. Moral campaigns need money and even the most sympathetic Methodist wants his neighbor to hear the click of his dollar in the collection plate. It is a well known fact, incidentally, that those Methodist churches whose collection plates have pieces of velvet at the bottom of them are the poorest, a circumstance duly noted and rectified at the last congress of the denomination's Bishops. The necessary public reaction, obviously, cannot be got from raids on plays encouraging gambling, swindling and even murder, but only from raids on those which involve sensational sex of one sort or another. The reason for this is the same as the reason which makes one murder in actual life more engrossingly interesting to the general public than another and intrinsically just as interesting murder. Since the Leutgert affair in Chicago many years ago, there has not been a single murder case in America that has lacked a sensational sex motif and that has made the general public wait avidly at the street-corners for the newspaper extras. Without exception, the murder cases that have most greatly made the mob lick its chops have been those in which sex played a suggestive part, and the Leopold-Loeb case was no exception. An attempt on the part of the moralists, therefore, to suppress such a play as "Crime," for instance, on the contendable ground that it was subversive of law and order, would doubtless only cause the public to hoot. What the public wants is a good, hot show on the part of the moralists, whom it regards in the light of so many paid melodrama actors, and the moralists can only give it with the actual dirt that proceeds from the prosecution of theoretical dirt. The moralists are no fools; they know which side their bread is buttered on; they know what makes the front pages of the newspapers and what does not; they know that a yokel who has been told where there is a warm belly-dance will presently want to be told where is an even warmer one, and that he will gladly hand over his money for the tip; and they hence very sensibly and intelligently, according to their corrupt and hypocritical standards, go about their dirty business. To blame them for not going about it differently, and honestly, is to blame a shell-game operator for not using three peas.

§ 3

The late activities of the righteous in connection with the theatre would seem to prove once again that a playwright's characters may safely say anything they choose to, provided only that they do not, whether by gesture or act, visualize the subject matter of their discourse. Looking back over those exhibitions that the censors have objected to in the last thirty years, it is easy to see that what has dismayed the guardians of the public psyche is not what is said, however piquant, but rather what is done. The only exception in the three decades in question where objection has been lodged against a theme and not against stage business was "Mrs. Warren's Profession." In every other single instance, what has brought the mudlarks down upon a play has been a physical antic of one kind or another. Olga Nethersole's "Sapho" was condemned not for its theme and dialogue, but simply because of one unduly prolonged "Carmen" kiss and a scene showing the hero carrying the heroine upstairs to bed. Sadie Martinot's "The Turtle" attracted the attention of the moral police because of a two-minute episode in which the heroine was supposed to disrobe behind a screen, and Blanche Bates' "Naughty Anthony" simply because an actress crossed her legs at one point in the evening and took off her stockings.

Paul Potter's "The Conquerors" would never have had a voice lifted against it had it not been for the moment in which a German *Uhlan* seized a woman with deplorable purpose just as the curtain discreetly lowered itself. "The God of Vengeance" offended the smutsers because of the scene at the end of the first act in which a woman fondled a young girl with what seemed to be saphistic intent, and "The Clemenceau Case," years before, because one of the actresses showed herself for ten seconds in a mild approximation to the altogether. "The Demi-Virgin" got into trouble, so it eventually came down to cases, because of a single amorous scene played by an actress in an allegedly aphrodisiacal nightie, and "The Girl With the Whooping Cough" because of some love-making on a settee. Even in the case of the harmless music show, "The Black Crook," it was only the girls' tights that alarmed the celestial ambassadors of the era. "Countess Coquette," though it managed to avoid actual police interference, came very near suffering it because of the scene at its conclusion wherein the deserted Lothario listens at the keyhole of the door leading to the boudoir of the reunited husband and wife, and a flannel night-gown in "Desire Under the Elms" was instrumental in causing what trouble that drama experienced in certain communities. The dramatization of Tolstoi's "Resurrection;" which Blanche Walsh took around the country, was jumped upon in various cities because of the scene at the end of the prologue in which a man and woman sat down together on the edge of a bed, and Charmion's trapeze act, to come to that, was all right with the gendarmes until the lady removed her garter and threw it to the audience.

Take the three suppressed plays of a recent season. What really drew the eyes of the moralists to "Sex" was surely less what was said in it than that single widely remarked-on bit of stage business wherein an actor employed a Rabelaisian gesture to indicate a certain anatomical virtuosity. "The Virgin Man," equally innocuous drivel, went on the moral rocks because of a single episode showing a young woman trying to tempt a youthful St. Anthony. And "The Captive," for all its homosexual theme, would, unless I am very greatly in error, have been permitted a free course had it been presented here as it was in France and not been circused by causing the actress playing the leading rôle to comport herself like a hoochie-coochie performer who had drunk a *Seidel* of yohimbin. Bourdet himself objected violently to any such sawdust-ring interpretation of the rôle which distracted an audience's attention from the drama and centred it upon the spectacle of a pornographic St. Vitus dancer.

It is always what he sees rather than what he hears that disturbs the moralist. The history of the modern theatre, with negligible exception, assures us of this fact. A dramatist may speak on forbidden subjects to his heart's content and he will be relatively safe. But the moment he dramatizes even one of his phrases in terms of concrete fact or action the gong of the Black Maria will be heard outside the playhouse. If this is not true, why is it that the moralists raid "Sex" and permit to go unmolested a play like "Saturday's Children," in which a father tells his young daughter that it would be much better for young girls to go out and have affairs than to rush into marriage too quickly, or one like "The Constant Wife," in which married women are defended for taking on lovers, or one like "The Road to Rome," in which a woman with a too fat husband is alleged to be justified in committing adultery with the first good-looking thin gentleman she encounters? Why is it that they raid any burlesque show offering the familiar frankfurter act and allow to be presented unhindered a play like "Crime," in which the young are romantically educated in successful thievery, or one like "The Pearl of Great Price," in which it is hinted that Cartier and Tiffany deal exclusively in the ὑμήν?

§ 4

Time hallows the sins of drama, it would seem, as it hallows the adjective *unpleasant*. Even the lowest dolt practising criticism would hesitate to dub as unpleasant the "Ecclesiazusæ," though the venerated papas do not hesitate still to bestow the adjective on "Ghosts," "Erdgeist," "The God of Vengeance" and "The Captive." To expect a dramatist to take an unpleasant subject and by some esoteric magic make it pleasant is to demand of him that he be a charlatan. That job is not for artists, but for quacks.

THE AUDIENCE EMOTION

The world may grow more civilized as the centuries pass, but I doubt that the emotion of the theatre audience in any period or over any stretch of time, however great, shares in the proportionate increase of civilization. The nature of that emotion and of its reactions may alter in detail, usually negligible, but I have a feeling that it is, in sum, pretty much today what it was in the beginning, and that its fundamental innocence will remain inviolate until the world returns to dust. This, of course, is like saying in different words that human nature does not change and that, in the mass, it responds always in much the same way to the various phenomena of life with which it is brought into contact. But there is a difference, and this is it. A theatre audience enters a theatre with the deliberate intention either of forgetting itself for a couple of hours or of being reminded of half-remembered phases of itself, of its life and of its dreams and despairs. In the matter of the former of these two psychological businesses it tacitly and volitionally requests of the dramatist that he render it other than it actually is, that, as the phrase goes, he take it out of itself—in short, that he treat it not as it really is, whether in habitual thought or feeling, but as it would like to be. In the direction of thought, it urges the dramatist to rid it of its stereotyped mental processes and, in the direction of feeling, of its conventional emotions and substitute for them new and more soothingly desirable ones. It comes to the theatre ready and willing and eager to be made, for the nonce, other than it is. At home or in the street it is in its divers elements content to be conventional, average, normal. In its reaction to the various affairs of the world it is even insistent upon this conventionality and this normalcy. But in the theatre, on the occasions I allude to, it pays out its money with the deliberate motive of constituting itself other than in its heart and mind it is. It wants a momentary spree, a night off. And yet, try as a dramatist will to give it what it wants, try itself as it will to make itself other than it is, it cannot. The so-called crowd psychology has nothing to do with the matter. The truth of the contention would hold were the theatre to be occupied by only two or four such persons. For the fact is that what is true of a thousand boobs is true of two boobs, and that what is true of two is equally true of the thousand.

Matthew Arnold may have been right about the world, but he was wrong about that part of it that is the theatre. The theatre, in so far as the emotional quality of its audiences is concerned, does not move. It stands still. The audience emotion follows always an absolutely cut-and-dried routine, varied only superficially, and any fine attempt to change its course must, by the very nature of God's magnificent images, come to grief. Across the centuries, the signal fires in Æschylus' "Agamemnon" evoke the same emotional response as those in Bronson Howard's "Shenandoah"; the audience's tears for Sophocles' Antigone when she seeks to follow her unfortunate sister are the same tears that are spilled over the girl in "The Two Orphans" who would do likewise; the laughter that was vouchsafed the drunken Dikaiopolis twenty-three hundred years ago is the same as that which is today vouchsafed the drunken Old Soak. We are asked by gentlemen who write books to believe that, where Sixteenth and early Seventeenth Century audiences viewed insanity as a comic affliction, modern audiences view it as a tragic one, but the gentlemen who write books have evidently—as I noted before—never been members of the audiences who have roared over a score of shows beginning with "The Belle of New York" and ending with "Chicago" and "Behold This Dreamer." We are also asked to believe that physical deformity, once regarded as extremely jocose, is no longer so regarded, and that, as a consequence, Mr. Glass' One-Eye Feigenbaum and Miss Loos' Spoffard *père* are instruments of profound grief, and that it is all that a modern sideshow audience can do to keep from crying out loud over the fat woman, the living skeleton and the bearded lady.

These general reflections occur to me in specific connection with a play called "Spread Eagle," by the Messrs. Brooks and Lister. It was the intention of these novices in the business of playwriting to persuade their audiences to gag at jingoism and the wars it periodically leads the nation into by

96

playing upon the emotions of those audiences with the various instruments of jingoism and then to make the audiences humorously self-critical, skeptical and ashamed of their own facile reaction. And what did these novices discover? They discovered that the aforesaid instruments for the furtherance of jingoism were so much more powerful in the audience's case than the latter's talent for self-criticism and skepticism that, far from making it catch on to its evergreen credulousness and susceptibility, they actually convinced it all over again. Though they suggested forcibly to the audience that they were playing "The Star Spangled Banner" with their tongues in their cheeks, and were showing it rousing movies of Our Boys going off to the front with their fingers crossed, and were making Liberty Loan speeches with a wink of the eye, the audience would have none of the derision and accepted the whole thing literally, and at one gulp. And what trivial success their play had, accordingly, was due not to what they put into it but what they tried and hoped and yet failed to keep out of it. What they endeavored to do was to show a theatre audience, in terms of

97

sardonic melodrama, the chicanery, mountebankery and nonsense of unthinking and blind patriotism; what they succeeded in doing was only to make their boob customers' hearts beat with the same old boob emotion when the drums got busy and the orators began orating and the flag was let loose. Their play, from any critical point of view, was a very bad play, but its badness had nothing to do with its failure to move an audience in the way they desired to move it. The same basic theme and the same central theatrical device are present in a good play by Galsworthy called "The Mob," and "The Mob" fails with an audience quite as "Spread Eagle" failed. Genius and hack alike inevitably fall before a mere brass band.

The one thing that a dramatist, however gifted, apparently cannot monkey with is the fixed and changeless emotional credo of the masses of the people. It is for this reason that satire is so seldom financially prosperous at the popular box-office. Now and again, to be sure, a freak play that assails the popular heart-beat achieves a moderate, freak success, but as a rule the play that wins the public is the play that in some relatively novel manner merely restates the ancient and time-honored emotional principles of the public. From the time of Aristophanes and his "Knights" to that of "Spread Eagle"—there are points of similarity in the former's Cleon, promoter of war, and the latter's Martin Henderson, ditto,—the public of the moment has been found to react left-handedly to the intention of dramatists who would whip its emotions in a direction that tradition opposes. A dramatist may play with superficially new ideas, philosophies and points of view. but down under them he must invariably cause to flow in a steady stream the old and tried emotions. Shaw is an excellent example of a dramatist who sagaciously appreciates the truth of this. Even a casual glance at his plays from beginning to end reveals his wise timidity in offering his audiences anything unusual or new in the way of emotional values. The Shaw dramatic canon is grounded upon a bedrock of grandma emotions tricked out, for the pleasurable deception of his customers, in the latest styles of philosophical and controversial haberdashery. Shaw simply asks his audience to feel the old feelings lightly instead of gravely; he never on a single occasion has asked it to alter the intrinsic nature of those feelings. There isn't an emotional note in any one of his plays that the lowliest boob cannot respond to safely and very comfortably, however much the boob may be horrified by the ironic counterpoint that Shaw synchronously plays.

THE KAISER'S HORDES

For all their pretence to the contrary, elaborately enunciated in tracts that seek to conceal a forthright knowledge of what they are talking about in a welter of terminology more suitably associated with architecture, bridge building, the navigation of sailing vessels and the manufacture of steam pumps, it is quite clear that what appeals to our adolescent dramatists about Expressionism is the ease with which it may be negotiated. Of all the forms of dramaturgy that have been devised in modern times, Expressionism, together with its blood-brother, Impressionism, is the simplest superficially to master, and it hence naturally has a strong appeal for those young men who wish to become playwrights without knowing how to write plays. Expressionism is, in essence, simply the emotional skeleton of a play, the scenario. It presents the outline of drama, substituting mere close-ups of faces for a near view of character and sudden, startling claps of thunder for the slowly gathering dramatic storm of human passions. The first essay that every schoolboy writes is always full of italics; they are his means of a forceful expression that eludes his unpractised pen. In the same way, Expressionism is a convenient subterfuge for such talents as are unable to achieve the intricacies and profundities of dramatic writing. It is to dramatic strength of expression what cuss words are to an inarticulate man.

If there are mind and experience back of Expressionism, as in the case of Kaiser or Toller or Hasenclever, we find the technique of expression subservient to that mind and experience and we get, accordingly, a measure of genuine strength and pulsating conviction. But the majority of the youngsters who lay hold of the dramatic form popularized by the Germans have neither mind nor experience, and consequently all that we get from their exhibits is the technical monkeyshine. Incapable of drawing character in its various detail, they foxily resort to faking it by throwing into relief only its high lights, wrapping themselves the while in the comfortable, protecting cloak of the Expressionistic theory and pretending that their abandonment of that detail is deliberate, when anyone with half an eye can see perfectly clearly that the abandonment is due simply to the fact that they can't help it. Unable, further, painstakingly to unfold a drama in all its devious complexity and to tell a story in the more conventional and vastly more difficult manner, they resort to the new formula with avidity, since it offers them the very convenient and lazy means of getting an effect by telling the plot of a play theatrically without writing the play dramatically. The theory that Expressionism's value lies in its power of suggestion, that it gives to the audience untessellated tiles and materials wherewith the audience may fashion the drama into a complete mosaic for itself and within its own imagination, is buncombe pure and simple. It does nothing of the kind. An audience gets from Expressionism exactly what Expressionism shows it on the stage; it gets three times more, as a matter of fact, from the actually much more suggestive and inferential drama of standard form.

Almost anyone with a slight facility in the way of literary composition can write an Expressionistic play, and one just as good as most of those our young men are turning out with such rabbit-like fecundity. The unhindered fluidity of the technique, the dismissal of the unities, the cinema-like hop, skip and jump, the absurd ease with which characters may be brought on and shooed off, the need only to indicate character superficially and the privilege to allow character to be identified in an entirely external manner and by such external means as manifold shifts of environment and intermittent comments by a mob of supers—these make the writing of Expressionistic drama even less difficult than the writing of music show librettos, in which some slight degree of consanguinity with the actual world must be preserved. A Georg Kaiser and an Ernst Toller employ Expressionism because it is a natural channel for, and even a natural outgrowth of, certain of their dramatic themes and ideas. No other form would serve as so apt a funnel for those themes and ideas. Our young men, on the other hand, lay hold of the technique as a quick-change vaudeville artist lays hold of a dickey with a diamond stud painted on it and a dress suit that can be jumped into from the back.

It permits them easily to give a show. It is a ready-to-hand method for them to parade as dramatists. Its eye-holding hocus-pocus, its off-stage jazz noises and its revue-like shifting of sets and pulling back and forth of curtains throw the audience off the scent and conceal the fact that they have nothing to say. Nothing? Well, perhaps that is going a bit too far. The young men usually have some such colossal thing to say as (*a*), that New York is a Juggernaut that consumes youthful dreams; (*b*), that modern business is a Moloch; or (*c*), that the syncopated gin life of today is bad for young girls. These great ideas that would cause them to be booted out instanter by any half-sober magazine editor to whom they submitted short stories containing them and that would go to make plays that would never get a reading from any manager, they set forth in terms of a set of scenery that looks like a waffle-iron and in the staccato form of tabloid newspaper headlines and thereafter posture themselves as very intellectual fellows. What they are are dramatic frauds.

NOTES ON THE MOVIES

§ 1

The promiscuously voiced contention that absurd censorship is responsible for the childish quality of the movies is sheer flim-flam. Censorship has nothing to do with it. I have investigated carefully the deletions that have been ordered by the various censorship bodies over a period of years and in not a single case would any one of the pictures have been perceptibly better had it been allowed to remain intact. The censors are idiotic, true enough; some of their recommendations are unbelievably asinine. But the pictures would have been just as bad if they had not meddled with them. The censors are the movie people's alibi. The latter groan that their great masterpieces have been ruined because an overly damp and prolonged smack or a Hun gouging out a doughboy's eye has been snipped out of them, when, as a matter of fact, the pictures have been given a modicum of gratifying subtlety, albeit unintentional, and a relatively increased merit by these very external interferences. Such pictures as the censors have horned into more broadly I find to have been out-and-out rubbish in the first place: cheap-jack sensationalism about prostitutes, social diseases and the like, on a par with the white-slave pamphlets got out by the moralists ten or more years ago, cheap-jack pornography and cheap-jack attempts at Continental sophistication. On such occasions as the movies have tried to do anything even remotely endurable, it is to be noted that the censors have very decently shut up. They didn't interfere with "The Last Laugh"; they not only let "The Big Parade" and "What Price Glory?" alone, but even allowed them to do and say things that, in the instance of the drama, would have brought the police on at a gallop; they didn't harm "The Grand Duchess and the Waiter" or any one of a dozen other such attempts to lift the pictures out of the nursery book. All that they cut out of the Russian picture, "Potemkin," were a few feet showing a wormy piece of meat and a baby having its head mashed in, both of which were nauseating and unnecessary and rid of which the picture was better than before. And if they made "Variety" foolish in certain hinterland communities by converting the old fellow's inamorata into his wife, let us remember that they did nothing of the kind in the larger cities and that one can't judge the movies by Podunk any more than one can judge literature by Boston.

The movie censors have, contrary to what the movie press-agents have insinuated into print, actually done no damage to a single reputable picture that I can discover. They have even allowed the movies a wider latitude in the matter of morals than is presently allowed the drama. The suppressed plays, "Sex" and "The Virgin Man," were baby fare compared with such freely circulated films as "Flesh and the Devil" or "A Night of Love." If you tried to put on in the dramatic theatre such seduction scenes as you may see daily at any neighborhood movie parlor, you'd land in the cooler before you could say Malevinsky, Driscoll and O'Brien. All that the movie censors usually do is to change a few subtitles, awful garbage in the first place, cut out exaggerated gum-suckings and brassière-squeezings that any artistically intelligent director would never have put into the film, and object to elaborations of incidents that every writer with an ounce of dramatic ability would himself recognize at once as utterly nonsensical and entirely needless. If anyone can show me a single comparatively worthwhile movie that the censors have spoiled, I'll believe this gabble about censorship ruining the movie art. But until the news is brought to me, I decline to become a party to the movie people's howls.

Every act of vandalism that has been attributed to the censors will be found to have been confined to what, when it started out, was already unspeakable drivel. All that the censors have generally done is to make the drivel more drivelish. They have done some things that make one laugh at their ignorance, but the antecedent laughter at the movie people's ignorance in the case of the same picture has drowned out a considerable portion of laugh No. 2. If they have cut out scenes showing a woman going through the pangs of childbirth, so would any imaginative dramatist. If they have ordered out scenes showing a woman sewing sentimentally on baby clothes, they exhibit a critical sophistication highly to be commended. If they delete scenes showing gas-house ear-biting, they do no more than any half-way competent stage producer would do. The movie ignoramuses are simply up to their old trick of passing the buck. The only ones to blame for the abysmal stupidity of the movies are themselves. The circumstance that the censors have stolen some small coins out of their purse can't conceal the fact that that purse betrays an unmistakable resemblance to a sow's ear.

§ 2

The movies will never be worth a hoot until the business end of the enterprise is absolutely and entirely separated from the actual producing department, and until nine-tenths of those presently in control of the latter are fired. Just as there never has been a magazine worth its salt that has got anywhere with a moneybags who meddled with its editorial conduct or one that has got anywhere when its financial, advertising and sales managers had anything to say about what went into its pages,

110

so will there never be reputable movies until the
money end of the business keeps its hands off.
What few fairly worth-while pictures we have had
will be observed to have been made by producers
independent of the Zukors, Mayers, Foxes and
other such financial padrones, by players or directors in command of their own destinies. I point, for
example, to Chaplin's "The Kid," Fairbanks'
"Thief of Bagdad," Griffith's "Broken Blossoms,"
and to "Nanook of the North," "Chang" and
"Stark Love." The other comparatively decent pictures that have come along from time to time have
been the result of continuous fights with the money
overlords on the part of directors and players,
with the latter triumphing by hook or crook over
the former's interposed hostility and objections.

To argue that the money men in the movies do
not know their business is ridiculous. They do
know it. The fact that almost every last one of
them, before he went into pictures, was either a
dinky fur salesman or an East Side push-cart ven-
der and that now almost every last one of them is a
millionaire, pretty well establishes the idea of
business acumen. What if they do waste money?

It isn't their money but Wall Street's, and that makes not them bad business men but Wall Street. They have got and are getting all and more that is coming to them, you may be sure. The trouble with them, like the trouble with most successful business men, is that they aren't content to be simply successful business men, but wish to be something else besides. In the case of the movies, they want to be judges of dramatic literature, producers, artists. And as not a solitary one of them, on penalty of death, could tell you the difference between "The Two Gentlemen of Verona" and "The Gentleman from Indiana," it is small wonder that their interference in the producing and acting end of the films has accomplished what it has.

§ 3

The moving picture will never really find itself until it divorces itself from the drama. Some things, of course, the two are bound to have in common, but the pictures presently lean too heavily upon stage drama and too little upon their own possibilities and resources. Again, all contentions to the contrary on the part of champions of the movies are hollow. Many of the innovations attributed to the movies, rendering them distinct from the acted stage drama, have not been innovations at all, but simply borrowings from the theatre. Griffith's so-called inventions, hailed some years ago as marking a new era of originality and progress in filmdom, were actually mere bald steals from the theatre. His much-talked-of device of fade-outs was originated and used years before by William Gillette in the plays he wrote, staged and acted the leading parts in. His flashbacks were nothing more than the old Drury Lane and Hanlon transparent backdrop scrims wherein theatre-goers of two generations ago used, while the hero or heroine was meditating in front of the grate-fire, to see scenes depicting the hero or heroine's childhood days and other such antecedent joys and aches. And his moving camera had its counterpart many years before in such stage productions as the Lilliputians' "Magic Doll," with the steps of its walker through the forest followed, as some of you will recall, in exactly the same manner as in Griffith's photography. Griffith was an actor; he must have seen and remembered all these stage tricks;

113

and when he became a director he took them over from the theatre with him.

But these are just tricks. The movie's real weakness lies in an attempt to cuckoo the drama's business and in the cuckooing to overlook and neglect what should be its own. The movie can never do the drama's work as effectively as the drama can, any more than dancing, even Pavlowa's, can, for all its trying, interpret music. The two are as intrinsically different as black and white. The movie must tell not the drama's stories in the drama's way, but its own stories in its own way. Now and again, it makes such an effort and the results point to what it may conceivably some day accomplish. "The Last Laugh" and "The Thief of Bagdad" are movie stories; the stage could not handle them; the movie can and does. So in the case of "The Big Parade," at least that part of it that Stallings confected, though certainly not the cheap imitations of stage drama that the director inserted into the script. In the instance of "What Price Glory?", those things in the drama that were finest on the stage are worst in the film, while those that could

114

not, because of the limitations of the stage, be shown in the acted play, are the best.

The moving pictures, I need not say, are simply pantomime with a *compère* in the form of printed titles. Their limitations and possibilities are the limitations and possibilities of pantomime, plus only an elasticity in scenic environment and background and a gift for ocular legerdemain that stage pantomime cannot hope for. The best movie actors and actresses are expert pantomimists all cameras aside. Thus, Chaplin is a moving picture all by himself before a camera gets in front of him and starts grinding, as anyone is aware who has seen him do his confidential pantomimes of French farce and so on. The dramatic actor, off the stage, is a dog without a tail; without the dramatist he is nothing. But the competent movie actor is a competent movie actor with or without a camera. The camera should therefore be reserved chiefly—in the director's mind—for the externals of the movie story and the story itself be directed solely toward those players who are valuable pantomimic funnels. But what is generally the present system? It is to take the movie story away from the expert pantomimists and give it to the camera, in other words, to convert the camera into a dramatist. Well, the camera is not a dramatist and can never be one, and hence we get the current movie blobs. You can photograph pantomime and you can, further, photograph drama in so far as it is pantomime, but you can't photograph drama of any other kind, that is, and persuade anyone but a half-wit. You can't photograph, with the greatest camera ever invented, metaphysical drama, or the drama that lies in luscious, beautiful, moon-struck words, or the drama of wit, or the drama that emerges from the conflict of ideas. And that is what the movies, though they don't seem to be aware of it, often pathetically try in their simpleton way to do. They foolishly and vainly try to do such things as "Romeo and Juliet," "A Woman of No Importance" and "Peer Gynt," when all the while the world of honest pantomime stands knocking at their door.

If I were the captain of a movie lot, the first thing I'd do would be to tack up a sign with the word SILENCE on it in letters six feet high and

116

not permit a single soul on the lot, directors, actors, camera men or what not, ever to utter a single word. Words get them into the habit of thinking and acting in terms of the speaking stage. They may not believe they do, but they do. It may sound foolish, but I'd make every one of them transact his share of the movie work in hand in pantomime, and I'd bank on the result. At its worst, it would at least be an improvement over the semi-callipygan stuff that the screen presently shows.

§ 4

The movie as we see it by and large at the present time is simply a stage play, its unities corrupted, stripped of its words, and made to show all the scenes and episodes that the dramatist has, with artistic economy, laboriously succeeded either in deleting from his work or in keeping off stage.

§ 5

If the motion picture ever hopes to be called an art by anyone besides the writers for the tabloid newspapers, it will first have to go into the back room, lock the door, sit down and take counsel with itself. And one of the first things it will have to persuade itself of will be this: that it will never get anywhere as an art simply by taking a generically static story and arbitrarily making it hop about, as it is presently doing. The mission of the motion picture is not to take what may be called a "still" story and give it legs that it doesn't need and that fit it grotesquely, but to take one full of movement and rid it of those static qualities that it might have, and unavoidably, as stage drama. However highly developed the movies may become, they will never be able to do such "still" plays as "The Lady From the Sea," "Night Refuge," "The Thunderbolt," "Candida," "The Father," etc., one-thousandth so well as the theatre can do them. But, on the other hand, they may take galloping tales, aburst with fury and alarm, and do them in a manner that the stage cannot. Yet the movies seem to believe that everything is equally grist for their mill. They have utterly no sense of discrimination and the result is what amounts to nothing more than bastard drama. The movies can no more do the masterpieces of drama than the stage can do the masterpieces of prose

118

literature, so let each concern itself with what it can do best. If the movies can't do "Hamlet," neither can the stage do Conrad's "Youth" or "Heart of Darkness." The difference between the drama and the movies is simply this: that the former knows it can't do such things and wisely refrains from an attempt to do them, whereas the movies ignorantly try to do everything and, as a consequence, cause a great nose-holding in the land.

§ 6

What is unquestionably the most feeble form of theoretical entertainment ever offered to American numskulls is to be found in the prologues and presentations currently on tap in the various movie palaces and cathedrals. Nothing like them has been seen in the world since the master-minds given to devising amusements for the images of God first invented tick-tack-toe. How the moving pictures themselves, bad as they are, have managed to survive these doubly infantile exhibitions is hard to figure out, for it is pretty well granted that to find anything more boresome than one of these presentations of prologues an audience would have to move *en masse* up to Bronx Park and watch the elephants getting a bath.

In New York, as in other cities, this movie prologue business is driving even the movie audiences crazy, which, I think no one will deny, is something of an achievement. On the Pacific Coast, a gentleman named Grauman is prologuing movie customers into a state of insensibility with acts showing Chinese emperors seated on gilt easels and Hawaiian dancers kneeling before Aztec idols, the while both are elaborately fanned with large palm leaves wielded by blacked-up Swiss acrobats. In the Middle West, the MM. Balaban and Katz are prologuing their trade stiff with South Sea scenes in which a number of chorus men dressed like Henry M. Stanley serenade a calcium moon with cornets, the while a troupe of mildewed hussies dressed like broccoli hoist their toes to right and left. And on the Atlantic seaboard, the Roxys, Boweses and Plunketts drive their patrons breathlessly over to the Erlanger and Shubert and Chanin houses with a series of exhibitions showing much the same sort of stuff that had already gone out of theatrical fashion back in the days of George Lederer and Tommy Reilly.

These movie presentations follow a cut-and-dried routine. One of the impresarios' big ideas is to hire six girls who can't dance and to conceal the fact by silhouetting the poor females against an opaque backdrop, usually painted to resemble a forest by way of making the girls' legs seem relatively thinner than the trunks of the trees. Another great idea is to paint the scene pink, rent a glass chandelier and two Louis XIV chairs, fit out the girls in hoopskirts and white wigs and call the result, "Minuet at Versailles on the Eve of the Fall of the Bastille." Still another gala notion is to engage a dozen chorus girls who are out of jobs, put fancy kimonos on them, have them toddle around the stage pigeon-toe fashion and program the gem as "In the Land of Cherryblossoms."

Just how the movie parlor managers figure that a very bad movie can be made better by prefacing it with an even worse prologue is something that only the deep minds of the professors in point can make out. Why a dreadful piece of screen mush showing a Hollywood cutie preventing the bursting

121

of a dam or a Hollywood ham wrinkling his brow like a great statesman should be immeasurably improved by introducing it with an act displaying a troupe of wenches in Greek nightgowns and called "The Temple of Pallas Athene" is, however, a problem for the rest of us less intelligent folk. If the impresarios were to introduce a movie with something or other good enough to make one forget the movie when finally it began to grind, they might be thought to have a little sense. But when they bore their audiences to death just before the really superlative boring of the evening is about to get under way, one may be forgiven for looking at them and tapping one's head in a significant and, I fear, impolite manner.

It is all very well to argue that these prologues must be pleasing to the movie audiences, otherwise the latter wouldn't stand for them. But exactly the same argument may be applied to an awful bellyache. As things go in this world, it is sometimes unfortunate that people have to stand for things that they don't want to stand for and that they would be a lot merrier without. If the moving picture audiences actually want the prologues, then I am ready to believe that theatre audiences actually want orchestraless theatres. The fact is that the movie audiences have to stand the prologues just as the theatre audiences have to stand cheap dinner gongs in place of musicians. They can either take it or leave it—and if they crave a movie (there are said to be such persons in the world!) or a play, they simply have to take it.

The movie prologues are the last word in entertainment banality. Up to date, there hasn't been shown one that hasn't disgraced even the worst movie put on on the same bill. And as disgracing goes, that may be said to be considerable disgracing. One and all, they are the sourest kind of dancing, pantomime and vocal hash, unworthy of a second-rate turkey show and as full of torture— even to a movie audience—as Torquemada's mother-in-law. The day that they are abandoned will witness a renewed wave of prosperity for the pictures. If they aren't, it will not be many years before the big movie palaces will begin to show figures on the wrong side of their ledgers.

§ 7

That the moving pictures must be mindful that their job is different from that of the stage may be practicably indicated by observing a single phenomenon in connection with both of them. In the theatre, artificial scenery representing outdoor views is an accepted thing. Audiences accept it willingly for what it is supposed to be. They permit themselves illusion, as Coleridge pointed out, not by their minds' judging a forest scene, say, to be a forest but in a remission of the judgment that it is not a forest. By all the rules, this should also be true of the movies, but it happens that it isn't. It was true in the beginning of the movies—when they were still a great novelty—but it is true no longer, as anyone who has studied movie audiences even superficially is aware. Show a movie audience today an outdoor scene painted on canvas and shot within studio walls and it will boo and snicker. It declines to remit its judgment and properly, for it feels—yes, even a movie audience sniffs the fact—that the business of the movies is to be absolutely realistic where the stage is ar-

124

tificial and (if I do not give the movie audience credit for too much discernment) on occasion artificial where the stage is sadly realistic. To put it in plainer words, the movies are commanded to take advantage of their possibilities in the direction of realism, possibilities that are plainly beyond the stage's range, and of their potentialities in the direction of artifice which, limited in the case of the stage, cause the drama sometimes unfortunately to be realistic against its will. Thus, in this latter regard, the stage can never show a fairy tale so convincingly as the movies, for the simple reason that, where the latter can achieve the complete air of artificiality essential to such a story, the stage at its best can only manage things half-way. On the stage, there must always intrude a refractory note of realism to dispel the illusion. The stage can evoke Cinderella's coach only out of painfully realistic mick stagehands; the movies can evoke it out of thin air. The stage can show a fairy princess only in the disturbing Broadway flesh; the movies can show her in misty intangibility. The stage, to speak of other than tricks, for all its intention must remain visually realistic when it tackles "Peter

Pan," whereas the movies may fully artificialize the eye. That the movies, when they in turn tackle "Peter Pan," succeed in doing nothing of the kind simply proves that they still so blindly follow the theatre that they botch what possibilities they have.

§ 8

It is a trivial point, and one beneath the dignity of an old professor, but I should like to inquire why those who have wondered over the pull of the movies and the audiences they have drawn from the theatre haven't noticed how very much better-looking the girls are than those on the stage?

§ 9

The extent to which the movies slavishly seek to emulate the drama, and in the act disembowel themselves, may be seen in their current practice of hiring playwrights right and left to work out scenarios for them. These playwrights, who, like everyone else, look on the movies merely as sucker-stuff to get easy money from, not only unload on the movies all the flapdoodle that they are too sensible even to suggest to the theatre, but have no

126

more idea, however willing and eager they may be, of the real requirements of the movies than so many Hollywood production managers. The number of fairly respectable movies that have been made since movies began are surely few and only one of these has been the result of a scenario prepared by a playwright. The rest have been made from scenarios manufactured by persons who were never near a theatre and who wrote for the camera purely in terms of the camera, even, in one case, where the idea of the scenario was lifted over from a play that had been done on the stage.

Of all the playwrights, American and foreign, who have been imported to Hollywood, only one, Stallings, has shown the slightest sign of appreciating the difference between the screen and the stage and, by that mark, he is the only one of the lot who has been at all spectacularly successful—even from the movie-mongers' point of view. The rest have been miserable duds. There is no more reason why a playwright should make a good scenario writer than why a scenario writer should make a good playwright. Even more playwrights during the last three years have come croppers in the movies than scenario writers like the authors of "Window Panes," "The Jay Walker," "The Woman Disputed," etc., have come croppers as dramatists.

§ 10

The movies are presently handicapped by the circumstance that they must all be fashioned with a single type of audience in mind, and that type the lowest. There are no different circuits of movie houses, as there are in the case of theatres, and hence a single picture must be made to appeal to all kinds and conditions of movie-goers in the mass. In the theatre, things are different. There are the divisions in the so-called legitimate circuit, the big-time vaudeville circuit, the small-time vaudeville circuit, the burlesque wheels, the little theatre chain, etc. Each of these can offer a specific fare, high or low, to appeal to the tastes of its own customers. In other days, there were the Syndicate circuit with its better grade of drama, the Stair and Havlin circuit with its second grade, the H. R. Jacobs and kindred 10-20-30 theatres with their knock-'em-down melodrama, and the stock company and other circuits. Theatrical entertainment was then, even to a greater degree than now, duly apportioned to the various strata of theatrical intelligence. But the movies never had such circuits or individualized playhouses and they haven't them yet. Consequently, a movie must be manufactured to meet the ten cent and two dollar trade on common ground. It succeeds in meeting the former.

The little theatre movement has begun to show faint signs of visiting itself upon the movie scene; already such playhouses catering to the minority taste are popping up here and there; and in them rests the artistic future of the films just as the artistic phase of the modern American drama found its birth in similar mangers.

§ 11

It is difficult to understand why the moralists have failed to include in their uplift forays those quasi-religious spectacles which are periodically displayed in our midst. If anything in the world can succeed in ridding a people of its belief in God and Holy Writ, it is surely just such blasphemous and ridiculous exhibitions. It is doubtful that a hundred plays showing the carnalities of forty-five years old actresses and imitation Englishmen can persuade even a congenital imbecile of the romantic aspects of wenching, but I experience some travail in believing that the man who has just seen Jesus Christ in the person of a Lambs' Club actor in a Hepner wig will go around to church the following Sunday with much of his erstwhile gusto.

The visualization of divine and Biblical subjects by the drama and the moving pictures has undoubtedly done more to hasten the spread of agnosticism among the peasantry than all the engines of doubt and disbelief that have got up steam in the last two hundred years. The subjects of faith and the objects of religious worship may, save in a traditionally conventionalized manner, be pictured concretely only at the expense of a diminishing and sacrifice of such faith and worship. Time and custom have hallowed the symbol of the crucifix, whether in marble or ivory or oils, and fine art has brought its beauty and imagination to the establishment and furtherance of the spirit of the divine materials it has made its own. But when cheap

130

playwrights and cheaper movie manufacturers, however lofty their purpose, lay hold of the same materials, they convert them into a species of pie theology and succeed magnificently in spreading a dangerous impiety and infidelity among a nation of dolts who must ever be kept in line by fear of the hereafter. It is pretty hard to believe that, after a journeyman electrician has seen Christ depicted in an exhibit like "Ben Hur" as a bunch of thirty-cent Mazda lamps, he will suffer quite the same humility that he did before. It is equally hard to believe that, after an advertising agent has beheld the Saviour in a show like "The Servant in the House" or "The Passing of the Third Floor Back" to be none other than a familiar endorser of Pelmanism, Muriel cigars and Lucky Strike cigarettes, he, in turn, will experience quite the feeling that he did previously. And it surely is no easy job to believe that, after thousands of morons have gone to such a moving picture as "The King of Kings" and seen the Son of God to be simply the actor who played the crook in "Alias Jimmy Valentine," to say nothing of the fellow who fell so comically upon his stern in "The Ghost Breaker"—it is surely no easy job to believe that these morons will not come away rather more given to humanitarianism than they were when they went in. Herr Lang of Oberammergau has at least never cavorted in Broadway detective melodramas and farces, nor has he had photographs in the tabloids showing him playing golf in Hollywood.

But more important than all this, in the direction I have indicated, is the picturization by the movies of the Biblical miracles. It may, with a painful stretch of the imagination, be conceivable that a half-wit may be deeply impressed by the spectacle of a dozen fox-trotting habitués of the Cocoanut Grove in the rôles of the Twelve Apostles, but it must strain the imagination to the breaking point to believe that he longer regards the miracles taught to him in childhood as divinely inspired after he has seen them reproduced by film parlor-magic, the secrets of which he is made privy to by all the movie magazines. Reading of the miracles in the Bible, he is awed. But seeing them duplicated by a Los Angeles bald-headed man in puttees, he is simply made sniffish. He is like a child who regards his father as a great man when the latter pulls a rabbit out of a silk hat and whose faith in his parent's supernatural powers quickly vanishes when he later discovers that the hat contains a black velvet pocket in which the rabbit was concealed. Suckers no longer fall for the shell game after they know how it is done. And the movie devotee, being apprised of the fraudulent way in which the miracles are transfered to the screen, presently persuades himself that the miracles of old were negotiated in some equally fraudulent manner.

As I have hinted, the rank and file of the people must be kept in line by the police, whether mundane or celestial. A people that didn't believe in an Almighty God might constitute an intelligent nation, but it would prove a very tough customer to handle. At least one policeman would be needed to look after every single citizen, and the jails would have to be enlarged daily. The pseudo-holy plays and moving pictures are gradually converting former believers into skeptics, and skeptics, by a recognizably natural process, into criminals of one sort or another. All that China needs to disillusion it, solidify it and make it a formidable military power is for Cecil de Mille to go over there with some fat movie actor and make a super-spectacle with him in the rôle of Buddha.

§ 12

The theatre need not be worried over the Vitaphone, the mechanical invention which synchronizes the movies and human speech. If there is any worrying to be done, it is the movies that should do it. For if the Vitaphone or its like is ever adopted generally by the movies, it will not be long before the galleries of the legitimate theatres are again filled with the class of individuals who deserted them some years ago for the films.

The Vitaphone is an interesting device, despite certain crudities that still exist in it, crudities that will doubtless be eliminated as time goes on. It does succeed in dovetailing speech and music with the movements of persons on the screen, and dovetailing them exactly. Its words and its tones are identical in time with the opening of persons' lips and the movement of violin bows. It still betrays an audible mechanism and it still possesses no light and shade; it is deafening. It makes the actor, the

singer and the musician alike so many boiler fac-
tories. But that is not the point. The point, rather,
is that, aside from its commercial value in certain
short-reel subjects, such as an opera singer doing
her bit or a politician exuding the usual platitudes
or a musician making pretty sounds, it will bring
to the motion picture exactly the thing that the motion picture should have no use for, to wit, the
human voice, and that, further, once it brings it,
the motion picture will have a difficult time holding
its own even among the jays who now make it the
profitable institution it is.

If the Vitaphone gets its deadly hold on the
movies, it won't be long before the latter's current
millionaires are driven back to their former pants
and delicatessen businesses. It is, of course, conceivable that once in a great while, once the ma-
chine is perfected, a reputable talking picture may
be made by hiring expert legitimate actors to enact
a first-rate legitimate drama for the articulate
screen. But even that is shadowed o'er with doubt,
for moving picture audiences would care no more
for, say, "Hamlet" thus done than "Hamlet" audiences would care for Miss Gloria Swanson in one

of her present masterpieces. Furthermore, since the actors who appear in the movies, even the very best of them, are pantomimists rather than dramatic performers, any effort to make them articulate would be not only paradoxical and absurd, but utterly futile. To expect a pantomimist, talented though he be, to be the possessor of a vocal organ capable of expressing all the shadings of dramatic speech is surely expecting a lot. The theatre, so far as I know, has not, in all its history, owned more than one or two pantomimists, pantomimists, that is, by strict profession, who were simultaneously gifted with the requirements of such dramatic speech. One may easily imagine, therefore, what nine hundred and ninety-nine out of every thousand movies would be like once the Vitaphone recorded and duplicated the voices of their performers. The result, one allows one's self to believe, would be like so many phonograph records of a Brahms concerto played by a speak-easy orchestra.

To wish the movies to be articulate is about as sensible as wishing the drama to be silent. The movies are designed for pantomime, nothing more. The titles that they generally employ, despite the

criticism of them, are legitimate for the same reason that the program synopses of stage pantomimes
are. It is all very well to pretend that pantomime
should be made so lucid by gifted performers that
any one can tell what it is meant to convey, but
for one such pantomime, or movie, there are a
hundred that need the assistance of the printed
word to make them properly clear. If a drama has
a program, why shouldn't a pantomime have a program also?

But—imagine such a pantomime as "L'Enfant
Prodigue" with articulate pantomimists, with words
accompanying the actions! That is precisely what
the mechanical gentlemen who are responsible for
the Vitaphone are eager to bring about. It would
be not more ridiculous for them to invent a ma-
chine to give a Rodin sculpture, say, the semblance
of movement. The movies have succeeded among
the peculiar audiences they cater to for exactly the
same reason that the tabloid newspapers have succeeded among the peculiar audiences they, in turn,
cater to. Both have, for the greater comfort of
their illiterate publics, boiled down the number of
words to a minimum and substituted readily com-

prehensible pictures in place of less easily comprehensible speech and type. The moving picture fortunes have been built upon the sagacious business theory of showing the boobs everything and telling them nothing. As Barnum catered to the public's eye and got rich, so have the movie magnates catered and got rich. To the producers of fine drama who cater to the public's ear, both Barnum and the movie magnates have willed the poorhouse,

The regular and enthusiastic movie patron is a person upon whom a strain may be placed only at the risk of losing him. When he is asked to use his eyes, that is enough. To bid him use his ears as well and coincidentally his intelligence—or at least that modest share of intelligence that is demanded to assimilate dramatic speech—is to ask the impossible. He likes the movies as they presently are for the simple reason that they impose not the slightest tax upon his imagination. All that he has to do is to open his eye, occasionally at least, and allow the screen balderdash to impress itself easily and casually upon his half-conscious retina. Words would change this acceptable situation, and enormously. The spoken word demands attention, not the semi-attention that pantomime demands, but taut attention. There is something commanding, challenging, about the human voice. And, in addition, there is something that calls for a degree of understanding. If the Vitaphone were to stick to words of one syllable, the movies might use it to some advantage. That is possible. But the moment it went in for words of two or, on gala occasions, three, Mr. Adolph Zukor would have to sell his twelve Rolls-Royces and 82-carat diamond suspender buckles, learn English, and go back to work.

LITERATURE AND DRAMA

The contempt exhibited by literary men for drama on the ground that drama, because of the intrinsic nature of the theatre, cannot be literature is analogous to a contempt that architects might affect for music on the ground that it cannot be made out of bricks. Aside from the painfully obvious fact that great drama actually is literature, and great literature, the literary gentlemen conveniently overlook the second and even more painfully obvious fact that the circumstance that drama may not necessarily be literature is no more valid criticism of it as art than the circumstance that literature need not necessarily be dramatic is valid criticism against literature as art.

Of all artists, literary men are the most self-sufficient, snobbish and, generally, the least catholic and critically sagacious. Whimsical fellows, they look scornfully upon a dramatist who must perforce resort to such ignoble and inartistic devices as the condensing of a character's lifetime into an arbitrary two hours while they themselves enjoy all of two hundred pages, which take two hours to read, for the same purpose. They laugh at the arbitrary demands of the stage in the matter of curtain falls, while they agreeably forget the arbitrary demands of the novel in the matter of chapters or similar necessary furloughs for the reading eye. They speak from a superior vantage point of bad actors, and overlook bad type-setters, bad proof-readers, bad binders. They think of theatre audiences, and double up as with a colic; but they do not recall that nine out of every ten persons who read their own work are similar bounders and pickleheads.

This attitude toward the drama on the part of literary men may easily be explained. It derives from their own inability to write drama when they try their hands at it and a subsequent attempt to apologize to themselves for that failure with the reassuring remonstrance that drama must be a very low art form, else they would be able to master it. It seems to be the literary craftsman's idea that drama is child's play, something to be taken up, largely as a joke, when his own more serious and important and difficult work is done. He does not realize that the two arts are as far apart as sculpture and painting. Thus, an Arnold Bennett observes loftily that any proficient *littérateur* can write a good play with one of his hands tied behind his back and his eyes blindfolded—and turns out such stuff as "Polite Farces," "Cupid and Common Sense," "What the Public Wants," "The Honeymoon," "Mr. Prohack," "Sacred and Profane Love" and "Milestones." The best that Frank Harris can manage is a "Mr. and Mrs. Daventry," which is to his literary canon what "Papa Loves Mama" is to "Andromache." Huneker, a champion of literature at the expense of the poor drama, tried to write a play called "Chopin" with sad results, and Sinclair Lewis is the author of "Hobohemia" and another opus, "City Hall," that shall be enveloped in a polite silence. Dreiser would doubtless be loath to have anyone speak of his "Hand of the Potter" in the same breath with "Sister Carrie," "Jennie Gerhardt" and other of his novels; and H. G. Wells is responsible in part for "The Wonderful Visit." George Moore, a great scoffer at drama and one who has looked on it as being of a piece with making mudpies, when he condescendingly tried his skill at it succeeded in producing only a "Coming of Gabrielle" and a "Strike at Arlingford." Heinrich Mann's literary talent gives birth to a "Die Grosse Liebe"; and Gustav Frennsen's to a "Sönke Erichsen." What Knut Hamsun's plays are like, I don't know; I haven't read them; but I hear that they are very bad. Henry James' attempt to make a play out of his novel "Daisy Miller" is still a dolorous memory, as is his "Guy Domville," and Joseph Conrad's "One Day More" is, considering Conrad, pathetic. David Graham Phillips, after much sincere trying, could manage only "The Worth of a Woman"; and Hergesheimer, after two separate attempts, appears to have given up. The short comedies and farces of William Dean Howells are of puny dramatic merit; Bret Harte's "Two Men of Sandy Bar" is drivel; and Robert Louis Stevenson's and W. E. Henley's attempts, "Deacon Brodie" and "Admiral Guinea," are equally drivel. No need to multiply the list; dozens upon dozens of additional instances will readily occur to you, both of yesterday and today.

The legitimate exceptions are few. Galsworthy, for example, is by his own confession a dramatist first and a novelist second: the dramatic form is closest to his heart. So with Maugham, though his plays are far beneath the quality of his novels. Thomas Hardy lately tried to make a dramatization of his "Tess of the D'Urbervilles" and failed to make one that was anywhere nearly so good as the antecedent one made by a more experienced theatrician.

The difference between a novel and a drama is the difference between music read and music played. The novelist peoples the imagination with ghosts; the dramatist peoples the eye and ear with living, moving forms and voices. This difference the literary man turned playwright seldom perceives, and as a result the drama that he fashions often too greatly neglects the eye and ear in favor of an over-taxed (and under-supplied) theatrical imagination. I speak here, of course, of the literary man who approaches the dramatic form seriously and not merely as a means to hornswoggle the box-office out of a bit of change. In the average play of the literary man, one can, in one's mind's eye, see the book leaves turning with the movements of the stage characters. One feels that the characters are reading their lines rather than speaking them. The dramatic personages move less in terms of sentences than in terms of paragraphs. They are less types than typography. A shoemaker should stick to his last. The composer of "Parsifal" is ill at ease in "Religion und Kunst"; the painter of the "Cenacolo" is lost when he woos the art of the composer; the author of "Romeo and Juliet" sloshes around uncomfortably in Ben Jonson's sock and buskin; the confector of the "Essays of Elia" only brings down a deserved booing upon himself when he confects a "Mr. H."

Of the several recent instances of the condescension of literary men toward the drama that have come to my notice, none is more illuminating than that of the gifted Mr. Aldous Huxley. Mr. Huxley makes known his airy disdain in an essay called "Why I Do Not Go to the Theatre." The title, considering the ancient point of view which the essay sets forth, would be vastly more pat had the author omitted its first word. For the theatre which Mr. Huxley so contumeliously discourses upon obviously belongs to the early eighties.

Let us glance briefly at a few of our friend's antiquated opinions. First, that "the popular conventions are accepted in the theatre at their face value without any attempt being made to discover the psychological realities which lie behind them." Brushing aside as being too apparent contradictions of Mr. Huxley's horsehair-sofa viewpoint the plays of such present-day dramatists as Shaw, O'Casey, Toller, O'Neill, Pirandello and a score of others, let us sample the hollowness of his contention by descending to even the Broadway commercial drama of last year. I list herewith a number of plays that, during that season alone in the New York theatre, turned the popular conventions inside out and at least tried to make the very attempt which Huxley denies is ever made: "The Home Towners," "Sour Grapes," "Sandalwood," "The Captive," "The Good Fellow," "God Loves Us," "Gentle Grafters," "This Was a Man," "The Constant Wife," "The Silver Cord," "Lady Alone," "Inheritors," "Mariners," "Spread Eagle" and "The Second Man." During the same period, there were produced on Broadway such equally contro-

verting examples of modern drama as the "Naked"
and "Right You Are" of Pirandello, etc.

"There are only two kinds of love on the stage—
the pure and the impure," continues Huxley in
defence of his non-theatregoing attitude. "No hint
is ever dropped that in reality sacred and profane
love are inextricably mixed together; it is never
so much as whispered that there may be a great
many varieties of both kinds." Need I bring to our
friend's notice a hundred and one modern plays
that must make his statement ring loudly with
foolishness, such, for example, as Porto-Riche's
"L'Amoureuse," certain of Arnold Bennett's later
comedies, d'Annunzio's "La Città Morta," Capus'
"L'Oiseau Blessé" and "Les Passagères," Strindberg's "The Dance of Death" and O'Neill's deriva-
tive "Welded," Sudermann's "Das Blumenboot,"
Schnitzler's "Zwischenspiel" and "Der Ruf des
Lebens," and Lenormand's "Simoon"? "On the
stage," concludes Huxley, "love is, moreover, always a function of the loved object, dependent exclusively on the blonde curls and the virtue of the
heroine, the black shingle and the alluring impurity

147

of the villainess. No allowance is ever made for the lover's state of mind and body. If there is one thing (on the other hand) that the novelist's exploration of reality has made abundantly clear, it is that love is, to a great extent, the product of the lover's imagination and desire and that it has comparatively little to do with the qualities of the beloved." It appears that Mr. Huxley is completely unaware of a multitude of plays like Schnitzler's "Countess Mitzi," Sudermann's "The Three Heron Feathers," Barker's "The Madras House," Strindberg's "To Damascus," and the various Guitry and Dieudonné comedies, to mention but a few that come readily to mind.

WRITERS OF PLAYS

§ 1

The major portion of the drama of Pirandello consists in a kind of metaphysical masochism. The Italian lays hold of a philosophical paradox and derives an intense orgastic pleasure from belaboring himself with it. Where Shaw takes the same paradox and uses it sadistically upon his audience, his Latin contemporary bares his own flesh to it. In his ability to laugh at his self-imposed torture lies the latter's genius.

The technique of the outstanding Pirandello drama is that of a pilosophical detective play, with Truth as the mysterious and evasive culprit and with all the characters of the play as sleuths. The play called "Right You Are If You Think You Are," for example, is typical of the leading elements in the Pirandello canon. As a *tour de force* in mystification, it must rank as a noteworthy achievement. Composed of materials that are essentially of dubious dramatic value, it is so ingeniously contrived that time and again when it seems that the whole structure must be on the point of collapsing, the uncommon wit of the author astonishes one with its jugglery of the theme back into renewed life. When the curtain falls on the first act, that theme strikes one as having been rounded out; there seems to be little that the playwright can bring to it to sustain it further. Yet the second act no sooner gets under way than what appeared to be a complete statement and relative solution of the theme is seen to have been but dexterous preparation. The same impression persists after the fall of the second curtain only to be dissipated by the rise of the third. The fault of the play theatrically, as with the bulk of the author's work, lies in its prolonged and unrelieved argumentation. It is mentally dramatic, but, after all, the theatre calls for the use of the eye as well as the ear, and the Pirandello drama has the air of being written for intelligent blind men. I do not make a point of mere physical action, plainly enough; what I mean is that Pirandello seeks to dramatize abstraction in terms of abstraction rather than in terms of theatrical concreteness. One sees his characters move about the stage, but the movement always impresses one as having been wrought by the stage producer rather than by the dramatist himself. For all that it matters, the actors might just as well be wooden dummies and their lines spoken by a ventriloquist.

Pirandello's favorite theme is the shadowy line that separates and distinguishes truth from fantasy, what is real from what is not real, and what is believed to be fact from what may conceivably not be fact at all. His method of presenting this theme dramatically is to lift it completely clear of the drama as we generally recognize it and to play it like an old-time minstrel show, without castanets and tambourines, but with the conventional interlocutor at centre interrogating in turn the performers seated to his left and right and commenting whimsically upon their replies. In "Right You Are If You Think You Are," for instance, the interlocutor is clearly identified in the person of Lamberto Laudisi, who, throughout the main portion of the play, sits elegantly aloof from the other metaphysical minstrels, periodically inquires of each of them the philosophical equivalent of "Who was that lady I seen you on the street with?" and upon each metaphorical reply that that was no lady, that was my wife, lifts his eyebrows quizzically and observes slyly that the minstrel addressed only thinks it was his wife as, under the laws of certain States and countries, no marriage would be recognized and hence the imagined wife was actually nothing more than the lady initially alluded to.

Where Shaw possesses the most agile mind in contemporary drama, Pirandello possesses beyond question the trickiest. In the matter of philosophical paradox there is no one like him in the field of modern dramatic writing. It is not, however, a mere superficial trickiness, but one that springs from a shrewd combination of introspective wisdom and a profound cynical humor. The virtue of Pirandello lies in the quality of his meditations and conclusions; his weakness in his failure thus far to evolve a thoroughly satisfactory species of dramaturgy to quicken them into consistently holding theatrical exhibitions. The greatest admirer of the Italian has difficulty in reconciling his considerable intellectual

152

interest in Pirandello's stage with his relative theatrical disinterest. The theatre, after all, is a place where ideas must not merely live but must also move. The ideas of the theatre of Pirandello are alive, as healthy human beings dreaming interesting dreams in their sleep are alive, but they are not dramatized in terms of their waking hours. Critics of the printed drama may justifiably take the opposite point of view, but critics of the theatre who do not confound a merely unusual and startlingly novel theatrical evening with sound and lastingly effective acted drama cannot help but deplore the circumstance that allied to the engaging Pirandello mind there is not the theatrical craft of some such worker in the sociological and economic phases of the Pirandello what-is-truth motif as John Galsworthy.

§ 2

The chronic sentimentality of James Matthew Barrie finds its most brilliant illustration in the play called "What Every Woman Knows." In the character of Maggie Wylie, Barrie presents his idea of a shrewd, discerning and canny little Scot female who, by a sedulous exercise of her qualities of understanding, observation and wit, manages to hold her husband after a long, hard battle not only with a woman rival but with the obtuse fellow himself. Dodge after dodge, wile after wile, tear after tear this Maggie is brought of apparent necessity to indulge in that the man of her heart may not wander from her. Time and again the odds seem against her, odds too heavy for her to surmount. And on each occasion Barrie comes to her rescue with some sort of impassionable device. What he contrives in sum to present, accordingly, is a character who is ever mindful that she is a stage actress and who, for all her alleged and heavily insisted upon canniness, is very little the shrewd woman out of life and actuality that Barrie would have us believe her to be. There was a simple and very natural and most efficacious way for Maggie Wylie to hold her husband, and that way was to have a baby. But that would have been the way of a real Maggie Wylie, and Barrie was, as always, concerned only with a stage character.

The sentimentality of Barrie is, of course, an old

story. With great skill, he permits nothing to stand in the way of it—not life, not reality, none of the hard truths of the world. His characters are for the most part marionettes with human hearts, but with heads filled only with sawdust and good theatrical dialogue. His talent consists in making an audience centre its entire attention upon these arbitrarily inserted hearts and thus making it unconscious of the complete absence of rationality in the characters. The technique of such a dramatist as Shaw is just the opposite; he cleverly distracts attention from his characters' lack of emotion, and so avoids commercial theatrical disaster, by making an audience centre its entire attention upon what the characters are thinking. Barrie's success as a popular playwright is due to his cunning in presenting sentimentality in relatively new stage terms. He lays hold of ancient sugars and molds them into novel and pretty candies. It is this trick that deceives all his audiences and most of his critics. They mistake for sound sentiment what is merely a statement of commonplace theatrical sentiment in an ingeniously fresh theatrical manner.

§ 3

Each reappearance of George M. Cohan on the theatrical scene leads one to speculate again on the peculiar neglect of him by those gentlemen who produce thick books on the history of the American drama. It is the practice of these gentlemen to devote long chapters to such figures as Nathaniel P. Willis, Mrs. Sidney Bateman, Clifton M. Tayleure, Augustus Thomas, William Vaughn Moody and other such writers whose actual influence on the native drama has been approximately that of Charles K. Harris on Richard Strauss, and to pass over Cohan casually with a paragraph or two, allowing that, while he has written some amusing Broadway stuff, he is a negligible quantity in any consideration of the American drama. Yet George Cohan, I believe, has exercised a greater influence on the American drama of the last twenty-five years than any other of his fellow craftsmen. I am not considering here the point whether that influence was a good one or not a good one; it is the fact of the influence that alone concerns me. Cohan's mark is seen upon so many American plays that one can't count their number. A whole train of playwrights has sprung up in his wake, some of them improving upon him, many of them failing lamentably to capture his tricks. He originated a type of entertainment that, in one detail or another, has been copied time on end. In play after play one sees the influence of his racy approach to character, of his technique and of his viewpoint. One of these days I may prepare a family tree of the Cohan plays, indicating the many direct descendants of each of them. "Seven Keys to Baldpate" has at least forty, "Wallingford" at least sixty, and "Running for Office" so many I shall have difficulty in remembering them. Think of the imitations of "The Governor's Son," of "Forty-five Minutes From Broadway" and of some of his later pieces! He has colored the American drama of a certain kind in a score of directions, quite as Eugene O'Neill, on a higher level, is beginning to color that drama in other of its aspects today. Any volume on the history of dramatic writing in America that omits a consideration of Cohan's influence is like a book on Briand that makes no mention of France.

157

§ 4

"One Day More," the late Joseph Conrad's try at the dramatic form, demonstrates the great novelist's discomfort in a field of writing that was strange to him. Here, once again, we have the favorite Conradian theme: the crescendo and diminuendo of life's aspirations—the futility of all earthly things —the travesty that lies deep in the heart of hope. Here, again, is the sea with its beckoning finger. And here, again, is tragic cruelty the delight of Nature. But where, in the novel form, Conrad mastered these materials of human urge and passion and despair as no man mastered them in his time, in the dramatic form he manages to lay hold of and project only the scant outlines of them. The impression one takes away from his little play is of a theme too big for it, of a whale attempting to sit in a sardine can.

Although Mr. Galsworthy appears in a criticism of the play published in one of the London journals to believe otherwise, I can't persuade myself that Conrad did not prepare himself for the writing of this, his first play, by giving ear to an oracle or two on the subject of how plays should be written. An investigation of the Conrad library would, I venture, have revealed a book on dramatic technique, or a scrutiny of the visiting-card salver in the Conrad hallway a card inscribed with the name of some fellow interested professionally in the drama. The play shows an unaccustomed lack of ease and assurance on Conrad's part and I can only ascribe these to his difficulty in reconciling his own ideas as to how a play should be written with the ideas that he had gained from others, and taken with perhaps too much seriousness. The very opening of "One Day More" discloses a pursuit of one of the favorite and largely nonsensical injunctions of professors of play-brewing, to wit, that, in a one-act play, the writer must immediately impress upon his auditors by overemphasis what, in a three-act play, may be registered in a relatively leisurely manner. Thus, the blindness and helplessness of old Josiah Carvil is mentioned exactly eight different times in the first five minutes of the play. And a similar emphasis by repetition characterizes the manuscript from that time on. Conrad was too great an artist to be guilty of such childish practices, whatever the form he elected to work in; it must be that, from outside sources, he foolishly permitted himself to be persuaded against his better and uniformly sound artistic judgment. Mr. Galsworthy has said that the play is not a dramatist's play, but a literary man's. It seems to me to be rather distinctly a dramatist's play, the dramatist in this instance being a bad one. Yet so sure a story-teller was Conrad that, for all the obviousness of his play's structure and for all the essentially rickety disposition of his characters, his fable manages to distill some slight measure of the force he had in mind. There is a fine sense of the lonely girl's ache and desolation in the final moments of the play; there is power in the suggestion of the old retired coasting skipper's hopeless hope. And the sad melody of Conrad's eternal song, the song of the brilliantly colored, empty box that is life, sounds momentarily.

§ 5

In "Marco Millions," Eugene O'Neill answers tidily those of his critics who have long and obtusely argued that he is without humor, that he sees

160

the world invariably as of a piece with an undertaking parlor, and that his failure to perceive the various essences of the mundane comedy operates to make his drama unnecessarily glum and hence suspect. Yet though O'Neill has accepted these critics' challenge in this play, it must be obvious to most persons who have taken the trouble carefully to consider his antecedent work that, if ever we have had a dramatist who has been keenly appreciative of the derisory humor that lies imbedded in the heart of even the most tragic dramatic translation of life, O'Neill is that man.

When these critics of O'Neill speak of humor, they mean not true, deep and searching humor, but apparently only the surface humor of the theatrical stage. Their idea of humor would seem to be chiefly that species which is extracted from the superficialities of life and character, not that—that profounder and more withering and more eternal humor—which is distilled from the aspirations and defeats, the hopes and trials and disappointments of mankind. Of this latter humor, O'Neill is assuredly acutely mindful; it trickles out from the bulk of his work like an ectoplasm and vanishes, as such humor must in the hands of an artist, even as the spectator begins vaguely to be sensible of it; it is suggested, hinted at, never emphasized. Emphasis of humor often simply betrays a dramatist's failure to plumb deeply his complex theme, and his effort to conceal his shortcoming by laughing his audience out of a perception of the fact.

O'Neill is not a humorist, in the signal sense of the word? Then what of the bitter humor that flows beneath the top layers of "Beyond the Horizon"? What of the unmistakable and more apparent ironic humor of "The Hairy Ape"? What of the romantic humor of certain of his short sea plays, notably such a one as "The Moon of the Caribbees"? What of the permeating sardonic humor of "Lazarus Laughed" and "The Emperor Jones"? Is there no humor, rich, low humor, in "Anna Christie"? The circumstance that O'Neill's humor usually proceeds from mankind's deep perplexities and miseries and not, as is the more general theatrical situation, from mankind's petty moments of relative glee contrives to delude his less meditative critics. The latter wish to laugh not with their sympathetic and understanding minds, but with their jaws. When they speak of humor, they speak of external, not internal, humor. They fail to reflect that God often swathes the slapstick with which He rules the universe and directs the movements and destiny of mortal man in black crêpe.

The critics here, as is their custom, are simply deluded by labels. Call a play a tragedy and they will no more appreciate the devastating ironic humor that, like a critical eel, undulates beneath its surface, than they will detect the tragedy that undulates beneath the surface of some such comedy as one of Schnitzler's or Pirandello's. Yet consider, for example, certain of the tragedies of, let us say, Hauptmann. "Before Sunrise" is tragedy, but does not the dramatist offer his own humorous commentary upon it by bringing down his final curtain on a laugh? In "The Festival of Peace," he slyly criticizes his theme by predicating its turn toward tragedy upon an ironically lighted Christmas tree. What is "The Rats" but a comic *reductio* of the tragic central idea of Strindberg's "The Father"? What is "Lonely Lives" but a bitter joke at the expense of Platonic friendship? Is there not an obscene humor in the fight of the two women for Gabriel Schilling? What is Flamm if not a shrewd comedian; and isn't August Kreil simply a bladder with which the dramatist belabors the seat of Puritanism? A certain school of criticism, however, elects to be oblivious to such humorous undertones of tragedy and to fix its attention wholly upon the grim misery that proceeds from those undertones. It sees the death of Hamlet, but not Hamlet's antecedent skeptical humor before a world whose jig-saw puzzle makes mock of his efforts to solve it. It hears Hedda's pistol shot, but not her ideas of her husband. It feels the agony of Strindberg's Julie, but fails to feel the spirit of Saint John's Eve.

§ 6

While the drama may be many miles ahead of Jim Tully, I doubt that the theatre has yet caught up to him. He is too cruel, too forthright and too raw for an institution that, for all its progress, is yet in many of its phases, by virtue of its democratic nature, still an ante-chamber to the kindergarten. Tully goes down into the sewers of American life for his fiction and dramatic materials, and out of those sewers he fetches forth characters dripping somewhat too fetidly for the pleasure of the native æsthetic tenderfoot. When his "Beggars of Life," as fine a book of its kind as has been written in our day, was lifted over onto the stage, it was found necessary, after the initial performance, to doctor up the element of incest that the weak stomachs of theatre audiences might not gag at it. The novel "Jarnegan" contains stuff that has outraged many; certain of its phrases would make Petronius himself rush for the smelling salts. This is true also of "Circus Parade." And we find in the play called "Black Boy" still further indications that the last thing in the world that the stage can do is to hold the mirror up to nature and get away with it.

This "Black Boy" is, in its technical phases, a play as crudely wrought as is "Jarnegan" a novel. Tully misses all sense of form; he has no more finish, in the accepted sense of the word, than a medicine show; he grabs all the blinding scarlets of the palette in his fist and, with one smash, smears them flat against the wall, from which they proceed to drip in ugly splotches. As I say, form is lacking, but if there is a writer in America today who can lay hold of mean people and mean lives and tear their mean hearts out with more beautifully appalling realism, his work is unknown to me. This Tully is the Weyler in modern American literature. Even his casual journalistic interviews, the best interviews that you will find in the public prints, have the flavor of the king's utterances in Scene 2 of the third act of "Richard II." The simplest chronicle of a movie queen's rise to eminence is not complete for Tully save it include an account of the way her illegitimate Hungarian uncle bit off her mother's ear in a fit of delirium tremens, of the attempt made by the vice-presidents of the six largest moving picture companies to lure her into white slavery on behalf of the presidents, of the three or four directors who were mysteriously shot by other directors for trying to force their wicked wills upon her, of incredible machinations on the part of Jewish purveyors of Swedish bathing beauties to destroy her prestige by spreading innuendoes concerning her and a San Francisco Chinaman, and of the manner in which the proud beauty was cured of an Oriental disease only after years of mixing mercury with her gin. His stories of hoboes, yeggs, harlots, jailbirds, niggers, of all the riff-raff of humanity, crawl among the vermin in the cellar beneath the cellar of Gorki's "Night Refuge." Their lusts and oaths and miserable bravery sound in a bar-room bacchanale. For when Tully approaches a character, he approaches that character's soul only after he has first ripped off the last shred of his undershirt, torn off his trousers and given him a contemptuously critical boot in the rear. The fellow has about as much delicacy as an iron-riveter. But, when his job is finished, no one can say that he hasn't got the smashing effect that he has gone after. And what is more—and this is the important point—that he hasn't got that effect legitimately. He is often cheaply melodramatic; he is sometimes so loud that he is unintelligible; but, when the roar of battle has died down, he has got his man.

"Black Boy," as it comes to us in the theatre with the name of Frank Dazey, author of the gimcrack, "Peter Weston," significantly added to Tully's on the playbill, is surely not the play that Tully originally wrote. The play that Tully wrote, if I am any judge of him, estimating him from his antecedent work, certainly made no such compromises with an audience's tender feelings and prejudices. I point to a single example. The play tells the story of a humble Negro's dream of grandeur that lies in the title of heavyweight champion of the world, in the attendant wealth and power, and in the love of a white woman. And it tells then the story in gradual diminuendo of the toll of vainglory and dissipation and of the final vanishing of the last wisps of that dream in the discovery that, like all other illusions of this world, the white woman, whose arms hold in them the fellow's unreal Heaven, is only a high yaller. Or, at any rate, that was the story, unless I am in error, that Tully's play once told. But when that play came traveling into the timid theatre, things happened to it. An audience would resent the spectacle of a big Negro —and the rôle was to be played by an actual Negro—indulging in amorous contacts with a white woman, or one who it was persuaded to believe was white. Did not, forsooth, such resentment show itself when the theme of O'Neill's "All God's Chillun" was announced? It would be unwise to take chances. And so the script was duly altered to include two "plants" assuring the audience in the earlier portions of the play that the woman, for all her appearance, had colored blood. Obviously, the whole point of the play was thus got rid of at one swoop, and the eventual disillusionment of the central character deleted of all dramatic force. A number of other such changes are as clearly evident, all contributing to a weakening of Tully's original. Yet, weakened or not, and with all its crudity, this "Black Boy" is nevertheless a living, breathing thing. It has more vitality, more kinship with actuality and more reality of character than nine-tenths of the artfully tailored plays we get in a round of a theatrical year.

§ 7

The recent revival of "The Servant in the House" provided the present generation with a good laugh at the expense of those critics who eighteen years ago deluded themselves into believing it to be a very fine play and its author, the Rev. Dr. Charles Rann Kennedy, a dramatist of considerable consequence. The play is clearly seen by these youngsters to be an obvious and transparent piece of sentimental mush, a fact which was lost upon the critical gentlemen of yesterday, as were the other equally obvious facts that Augustus Thomas was a rank fifth-rater, that "Paid in Full" and "The Easiest Way" were mere Broadway trade-goods, that Belasco was at best an expert in trivial parlor magic, that George Ade was a hundred times more important figure in American drama than George Broadhurst, that George M. Cohan had other talents than flag-wagging, that Brieux was three parts charlatan to one part honest craftsman, that Mrs. Fiske was kinder to dumb animals than to the rôles of her dramatists, that Charles Klein was a dud, and that the little theatres then beginning to sprout here and there in the countryside might some day be something for very serious consideration. A glance at the critical standards obtaining in our midst in that gala era is fruity in illumination as to how completely addle-pated and idiotic dramatic reviewing can be when it tries hard enough.

It was from this school of criticism that the Rev. Dr. Kennedy gained the gold medals which have since turned out to be brass. Looking back at the estimates of Kennedy, one finds him regarded by the late papas of the critical art as something of a genius. His pulpiteering was confounded with sound drama; his juvenile and diabetic point of view was accepted as a likely brand of philosophy; his dark stages were looked on as being evidences of a highly lighted mind. "The Servant in the House," his first play, was received with a grade of respect and admiration reserved in this day for outstanding and brilliant dramatic talent. His second play, "The Winter Feast," was treated as seriously as if it were some gem out of the Elizabethan period. "The Terrible Meek," which followed, got columns of hearty grease. And "The Army with Banners" worked up our venerable friend Towse to such a pitch of enthusiasm that it took the entire staff of the *Evening Post* to calm him down enough to prevent him from bursting a blood-vessel. A consideration of these great art-works today is productive of a vast amount of impolite sneezing. All that one can discern in them is the pathetic and futile effort of a clergyman to be a dramatic poet.

Kennedy's technique consists in laying hold of some completely cut-and-dried theme, preferably derived in one way or another from Holy Writ, and in concealing its banality by announcing it in portentous theatrical terms. He gives his characters the sort of stuff to speak that one can hear any Sunday at an Ocean Grove, New Jersey, revival meeting, or at any Chautauqua conference, and then craftily directs the actors who play the characters to deliver that stuff in the voices of undertakers suddenly elected to the House of Parliament. In addition, as I have observed, he exercises the wily precaution of having the stage lights so low that the audience cannot detect the actors laughing. This mastery of hocus-pocus deceived the papas of fifteen and twenty years ago completely. Since the majority of them had estimated Ibsen and Gorki in terms of darkened stages, having been deeply impressed thereby, they saw no reason to be inconsistent and duly estimated Kennedy in the same way.

§ 8

The talented and generally astute Mr. Joseph Wood Krutch, commenting on the Guitrys and their plays in the *Nation*, goes to considerable pains polishing off the critical high hat, adjusting it becomingly to his brow and pointing out, not without a touch of professorial disdain, that they are on the whole, for all the fuss that has been made over them, unimportant. While I entertain a very considerable respect for Dr. Krutch's opinions, all that I can say as to his present one is that he is quite correct, and, saying so much, yet ask him in the same breath, what the hell? Why will otherwise intelligent critics persist in going on with this arch jabber about important and unimportant? It should certainly be obvious to them that, once one ticks off the relatively few dramatic geniuses in all the history of the theatre up to the moment, everything thereafter may very properly be put down as unimportant. Since the theatre began, there have probably been not more than a hundred plays which, regarded from the highest elevation of criticism, might be forthrightly designated as important; the rest fall into other grooves, are comparatively subordinate and, in the strict sense of the label-lickers, unimportant. If a critic of today were to confine himself solely to important drama, he would have very little indeed to write about.

The point, however, is that not everything that is unimportant (using the adjective in Mr. Krutch's sense) is, if he will forgive me the Hibernicism, unimportant. Critically, theatrically and dramatically, there is often a great deal to be found in what is undeniably unimportant, that is, so far as comparison with drama of the highest grade goes. Pinero's "The Magistrate" is certainly thoroughly unimportant in this respect, yet a fat book might be written tracing its influence on subsequent playwriting in the direction of the single device of humorous reiteration. The plays of George M. Cohan are unimportant in the same respect, yet, as I have noted, they influenced playwriting in America for many years as nothing else in their earlier day or, for that matter, their later day, influenced it. The least important and perhaps the worst of all the plays of Strindberg was the seed whence sprang the whole Expressionist movement, and an obscure two-act farce shown briefly in France fifteen or so years ago changed much of the character of farce writing that has been done since. The catalogue might be continued indefinitely, and carried back into other centuries. An apple changed the history of the human race, provided the world with one of its greatest heroic legends, and gave birth to a world-shaking scientific discovery. A thing equally trivial has often altered the course of dramatic writing. A German, whose name not one Anglo-Saxon critic out of a hundred has ever heard of, years ago wrote a negligible play that not one such critic out of two hundred has ever heard of, and in its train followed the wave of anti-sentimental dramatic sex that was to be hailed as revolutionary and that turned the Twentienth Century drama into entirely new channels. Nor let it be forgotten that the greatest drama the English stage has ever known was the direct flower, both in form and content, of the very least and most unimportant. It is not always easy to detect actual unimportance; the history of dramatic criticism is rich in illustration of findings that, read in these later years, are richer still in low humor. What may seem trivial at the moment has a way, sometimes, of turning out to be the opposite. The important work of even important dramatists has often been curtly dismissed as completely unimportant by befuddled and short-sighted critics.

But all this is beside the point I started out to make. That point was this: that, while Guitry's plays are undoubtedly unimportant, their very virtue rests in that unimportance. They belong not to the marble niches of drama's hall but to the unaffectedly charming, amusing and very delightful little by-corridors wherein, now and again, even the best and most serious of critics, for all their prevarication, like to disport themselves. They are of the little pleasures and gratifications of life. The theatre needs such things badly; without them it would die the death in no time. A theatre given over entirely to true masterpieces of dramatic art, night in and night out, would find itself converted into a dance hall or skating rink before many years had passed. Even a great philosopher wants to play pinochle once in a while. There is something wrong with the kind of critic who can see nothing in the unimportant things of the theatre. For they give to the theatre that which it must have or perish: the light moments, the light laughter, the little wayward gaieties and the superficial and consoling joys of a too thoughtful and hence miserable human race.

§ 9

One of the surest ways to make an impression on the men who review plays for American newspapers is to take a hokum hero out of a hokum drama and make him a villain. This simple procedure leads them to much enthusiasm over the playwright's "point of view," "force and originality" and "uncompromising analysis of human motives." Let any third-rate dramatist take a traditional character of the stage and, while preserving it intact so far as internals go, simply cause it to say *no* where formerly it said *yes* and, further, to act nasty where before it acted nicely, and the next morning you will find him hailed either as the logical successor to Bernard Shaw or as a writer with signs of unmistakable courage and genius.

This is the system whereby Mr. Sidney Howard, among others, has got himself to be regarded as a bravo of the first carat. It is Mr. Howard's practice to lay hold of the conventional characters of the conventional hick drama and make them seem alive by making them contradict what they have been saying on the stage, lo, these many years. The device contrives to bamboozle the critical gentry into believing that what is new is also authentic. Thus, "They Knew What They Wanted" got notices only slightly less ecstatic than a revue tap dancer simply because the revolver of the 10–20–30 melodrama was taken away from its leading character and because he was brought instead to accept philosophically the dirty trick that had been played upon him. Thus, "Lucky Sam McCarver" was greeted with a geyser of hooplas because its leading character was brought to comport himself directly opposite to the manner in which the same leading character had been acting in other plays for years, a circumstance which deceived the reviewers into believing that he was therefore closer to life than his old stage brother, when, as a matter of fact, he was nothing more than the spurious reverse of an already spurious Jerome K. Jerome stage dummy. Thus again, "Ned McCobb's Daughter" got under the susceptible mentalities of the reviewers. And thus, too, "The Silver Cord" set them a-twitter merely on the ground that it took the old gray-haired mother out of the lace valentine drama and showed her to be something of a nuisance.

This turning of venerable and established dramatic characters and themes inside out has got to be so transparent a trick that one would think it would no longer fool anybody. But it does. The reviewers still imagine that any old-time play stood on its head is *ipso facto* a good play. So-called novelty of viewpoint is regularly mistaken for sound and deep dramatic ability. Things have got to such a pass that all a playwright need do to create a stir is to take "East Lynne" and make Levison the hero instead of the villain, or to rewrite "Magda" as a comedy. Ever since Stanley Houghton got the reviewers by the ears by the simple expedient of stealing a line from Max Dreyer and making his heroine turn turtle on her old self, writers of plays have found the same reviewers easy pickings. Mr. Howard's plays are thus discovered to be interesting only superficially. Look into them closely and you will see merely routine drama arbitrarily made to thumb its nose at itself. It never rings true. One or two scenes are effective as mere novelty contrives ever to make such scenes effective, but in the main one can detect the playwright in the act of trying to make a dent simply by making faces at the Winchell Smith drama.

Mr. Howard does not lift his characters out of life onto the stage; he lifts them off the stage and in the process believes that they thus automatically become part of life. They remain actors, with all the idiosyncrasies and exaggerations of actors, parading ridiculously among real people. They do not live; they merely talk of living. They are spaghetti waitresses not out of San Francisco spaghetti joints, for all their say-so, but spaghetti waitresses out of stage spaghetti joints, mouthing in American slang the sentiments of young German post-war playwrights. They are self-made McCarvers come up not from the gutters of the mean streets but from the *papier-mâché* gutters of the Edward Sheldon drama. They are miserable New England women struggling ferociously to maintain the family honor not out of New England and humanity but out of a vernacularized paraphrase of the stage plays of Galdos and Sudermann.

§ 10

Of those writers for the American theatre who devote themselves to a vivisection of the theoretically tender passion, Vincent Lawrence, it seems to me, is the most consistently informed and intelligent. He alone, in the dramatic examination of the emotion known as love, approaches the subject with a shrewdly observant and adult head. I have heard him compared, in this respect, with Clyde Fitch. Such a comparison is nonsensical. Although he hasn't anything like Fitch's talent in the composition of plays, Fitch was a sentimental sophomore compared with him in so far as the handling of amour is concerned. If Lawrence could write plays as well as he analyzes his themes in his own consciousness, he would be a comedy writer worth reckoning with. But the trouble with him is that, once he has interestingly announced his point of view and sustained it adroitly with some of the realest dialogue being written today, his dramatic imagination gives out and his plays trail off into space. Even so, however, his field is his own among the native playwrights. Save S. N. Behrman in a single instance, none of them, in the dramatic consideration of love, courtship and marriage, has got anywhere near the calm philosophic sense that lies imbedded in such of his treatments as "The Ghost Between", "Two Married Men" (in part as brilliant a comedy as we have had in the American theatre), "In Love With Love," "Two Fellows and a Girl" and "Sour Grapes."

The American playwright who has concerned himself with love in its various manifestations has almost uniformly revealed himself to be either an over-sweetened ass or a sour indignanto. He has treated of it either in terms of soft waltz music or of pistol shots. Its sardonic loveliness, its irritating humor, its recalcitrant burlesque and its mirage-like glamour have evaded him, and all that he has been able, in his yokel way, to make of it has been a kiss in a Sunday-school or a seduction in a pigsty. Study the chart of love as we have got it in the American drama and you will find the sort of treatment of the subject that one gets in the women's magazines on the one hand or the tabloid newspapers on the other. A man loves a woman in a pure and holy manner, duly marries her, and the curtain comes down. A man loves a woman in an impure manner, does not marry her, and the curtain comes down with her in the arms of her forgiving fiancé or husband. A married woman finds her eyes wandering but eventually concludes that her place is with her spouse, and the curtain comes down. A married man cheats and his wife, declaring that what is sauce for the gander is also sauce for the goose, does likewise, and the curtain comes down. All is surface; the playwright never gets under it for a moment. All is actor stuff, as far removed from the truth, except in the matter of externals, as the two poles. These externals Lawrence takes, holds under a microscope, and dramatizes what he detects therein. His plots do not matter; they are at bottom conventional enough. It is the detail of observation and deduction that makes his plays, even though they are very far from the first quality, the engaging things they are.

"Sour Grapes," one of his latest efforts, is not one of his best. Placed beside "Two Married Men," for instance, it seems feeble. But the sharp nosing out of the phenomena of amorous reactions is present for at least two of its three acts. In the easiest manner imaginable, Lawrence lays hold of the stereotyped personages and situations of American comedy-drama and looks the truth into them. This truth is not always dramatic, employing the adjective in the Rialto sense, but it is the ground-work of reputable and important comic writing. Fine comedy is ever disconcerting to complacency. Now and again in his effort to make the theatre and life meet on natural ground, Lawrence foozles matters. His attempt to avoid drama and touch life, to remove theatricality from the standard situations and interpret them in terms of the living world, occasionally turns upon him and makes him, albeit unintentionally, doubly artificial and theatrical. Of this we have an example in this "Sour Grapes" when the girl about to have a baby by the man she loves rejects his proposal of marriage on the ground that his fancy is fixed elsewhere. Such a girl may exist in drama, but Mr. Lawrence will have to travel a devil of a distance before he finds one in actual life. Again, his notion that he has unearthed a new idea—the newness being thrice emphasized by him during his last act—in the philosophy of rekindling love by a mere pretence of rekindling it is hardly what he imagines it to be. May I refer him to the writings of Edouard Pailleron?

§ 11

Sean O'Casey's "Juno and the Paycock" is noteworthy for two very good instances of character drawing, for its measure of warm and comprehending humor, for its curiously effective handling, in a suspensive manner, of the character of the son of the Boyle household who has betrayed a fellow patriot, and for a brief flash of moving drama, toward the end of the play, in the boy's death at the hands of his colleagues' avengers. It is deficient in the trick of so assembling these virtues that the whole shall produce a play as meritorious as its component parts.

The price of O'Casey's imperfect manœuvring of his materials is, after the evening has passed its middle mark, tedium. Everything is on the stage to make a consistently holding play, but the materials are like a troop of fully armed soldiers whose commander is down with the measles and who accordingly hang around, their rifles cocked, waiting vainly for orders to move forward. Time and again, the smell of approaching drama is in the air and the nose sniffs in eager anticipation only to be disappointed. The first act proceeds smoothly and amusingly, centred as it is upon the character of the lying, bragging, lovable loafer, Boyle, quondam sailor on a coal-barge that never got further than Liverpool, but in his own tireless imagination and gabble a sea-dog among sea-dogs. The colloquies between Boyle and his bootlicking neighbor, Joxer Daly, are as diverting as anything you'll find in the playhouse at the moment. But once the flush of this initial act is over, O'Casey's fancy and dexterity give out, and, after a half-hour more, his play drops with an audible bump.

The failure of O'Casey to master his materials is readily discernible in the length to which he goes to conceal his dramatic nervousness in heavy exaggeration of dramatic and comic episode. Not only does he so overdo the burlesque song renditions of his characters in the second act and the tragic melodrama of his last act that these portions of his play lack all conviction, but, to boot, he so segregates comedy and drama that one kills the effect of the other. His second act is almost entirely in the low comedy vein and his third act, cut off from the other as with a meat axe, piles tragedy upon tragedy so exaggeratedly that it would take a professional pallbearer to profess any show of sympathy over his characters' plight. The impression is of a man stopping suddenly short in the midst of a comic story to tell the plot of "Œdipus Rex." Tragedy, to be convincing, must mount cumulatively and slowly; O'Casey directs it in the tempo of a rapid succession of unanticipated fire alarms. Within the space of a comparatively few minutes, he betrays his young heroine and gives her an illegitimate baby, causes her lover to swindle the family out of a rightful inheritance and run off to England, brings the son of the household to be shot to death in a gutter, separates husband and wife, desolates the home of his protagonists to the extent of removing its last chair, gives his central character delirium tremens, induces the young man who has planned to marry the daughter to sneak away, and suggests that the cause of Irish freedom is up a tree. His traffic in tragedy reminds one, indeed, of nothing so much as the familiar smoking-car story about the sorely harassed parent whose steadily augmenting family woes are brought to a climax by his small son Abie's unhousebroken deportment and who, at his wits' end, is informed by an old gentleman seated back of him in the day-coach that, unless he mend his Abie's ways at once, the old gentleman will make trouble for him.

In his later "The Plough and the Stars," on the other hand, O'Casey has produced a piece of work not less full of defective detail than his "Juno and the Paycock" but, for all that, a drama excellent in its characterizations, rich in an irony that reaches the heights of cruelty, and paradoxically powerful in lasting impression. Three or four of the episodes have the stamp of unmistakable dramatic genius; quietly as a cannon on rubber tires O'Casey rolls them toward the footlights and suddenly thunders them into the startled consciousness of his audience. As a surgical picture of the Irish, I know of nothing in drama or literature that comes anywhere near this play. That the Irish merely gave vent to catcalls and eggs when it was shown in Dublin is surprising; that they didn't bomb the theatre is even more surprising. O'Casey takes his people, themselves, their ambitions, their dreams, their pretences and their innermost philosophies, and doesn't leave a green thread in their chemises when he gets through. His clinical portrait is the most vicious thing in modern dramatic literature, but the viciousness is that of a deep understanding, a profoundly critical love and a prophylactic hair-brush swatting a turned-up child. His play is long, too long. As in "Juno and the Paycock," he doesn't seem to know exactly when to let go. The technique in both plays is much the same, although it is ex-aggerated in the one under immediate discussion. O'Casey busies himself leisurely with character for the first thirty-five minutes of each act, and then suddenly in the last five minutes recalls that, after all, a drama should have at least a little drama in it and belatedly dramatizes in a few moments the ambling antecedent business. The break is not too well dovetailed. The effect is of a Dutch concert disconcertingly interrupted by a pistol shot. Again, as in "Juno and the Paycock," the dramatist piles on the final woe to such an extent that a measure of persuasiveness is deleted from his work. His

189

wholesale murder, sudden death and general desolation are Shakespearian in every way but the com-
pensatory one of great poetry. The stage at the
conclusion of his tragedy resembles nothing so
much as the floor of a slaughter-house. Those characters who haven't been shot and killed are either
dead of tuberculosis, insane, in the last stages of
alcoholism or being led off the stage for no good
purpose. Still again, as in the other play, "The
Plough and the Stars" overdoes to the point of
irritation the vaudeville trick of repeating a word
or phrase for humorous ends. It was Pinero who
once pointed out the limit to which this device could
prosperously be used, and then topped it by one.
O'Casey tries to top it by ten or fifteen, and naturally fails. He also goes in once again for the
mispronunciation of words by way of getting a
cheap laugh, as in the instance of *chaos* in "Juno"
—and he repeats and repeats. But—when the play
is over, the effect the playwright has set himself to
get is as peculiarly and bafflingly there as the hair
in your nose. You carry with you out of the theatre a merciless, yet sympathetic, vision of Ireland
and its youngsters in grown-old bodies. You feel

the utter futility of a people and a purpose, the tragic ridiculousness of a nation of eternal children playing politics with loud nursery rattles and playing soldier with pop-guns. You look upon this picture of the Irish by an Irishman, one of the most articulate fellows on the Emerald Isle, and you smile and wince at the same time.

There isn't a character in O'Casey's gallery that isn't well-drawn. Some are superbly drawn. There is, for example, the carpenter Fluther, the alternately genial and bellicose souse who is constantly swearing off the stuff for good and who is as sharply perceived a study of an Irishman, down to the smallest detail of thought and act, as the drama has given us. There is the little old querulous Irishman, Peter Flynn, proud as a peacock over marching in meaningless parades in elaborate and meaningless regalia. There is the young Irish liberal and dreamer, constantly mouthing an ill-assimilated amount of sociological information; there are, in sharp, brief little strokes, portraits of Irish women and of Irish ballyhoos and of English militia men. Some of the episodes, as I have said, have the vital smash of kindly gunpowder: the scene at the saloon bar with Irishmen getting indignantly cockeyed while, outside the place and as counterpoint to the bibbing inside, other Irishmen, equally indignant, are haranguing their fellow countrymen to defend their immemorial rights with their eternal souls; the climax to the second act wherein, the political indignation reaching its zenith, one of the Irishmen lets off his accumulated martial steam by fighting another Irishman, both of them drunk, for an insult offered by the latter to an Irish prostitute's virtue, and then goes off with the woman for the night; the richly comical yet searching episode in the following act in which, with Dublin strewn with English bullets and Irishmen dying on every hand, the women make the practical best of the situation, news arriving of the pillaging of shops and stores, by taking a baby carriage, previously the subject of acrimonious dispute among them, and with true sisterly concurrence hustling off to load it with pink lingerie, white shoes, parlor lamps and other treasures out of demolished show-windows; and the final moment of the play wherein two English petty officers, with the results of carnage all about them, quietly observe that it is five o'clock and settle down to drink the tea that has been set out by an Irishwoman for her soldier husband dying somewhere in the gutter below the tenement.

§ 12

That the stage is the bourse of platitudes has long since been itself a platitude. The aim and perhaps the mission of drama are simply, through the instrumentality of art, to give platitudes a fresh breath of life and now and then, where possible, overtones of beauty. In the entire history of the theatre there has never been produced a play, great or puny, that had anything new to tell an intelligent audience. What newness drama may have had has been confined entirely to the newness of method and manner in merchanting ideas already familiar. The theatre presents age-old emotions in a fresh fashion; it also presents familiar philosophies in terms of unfamiliar mouthpieces; but it never presents a single new contribution to human thought.

In this direction, such an exhibit as the William Hurlbut play, "Bride of the Lamb," offers itself as an interesting clinical specimen, interesting not because it is an interpretation of life but because it is an interpretation of most of the religious plays produced since the beginning of the present century. The author has not gone out into the world for the materials of his play; he has gone into the theatres, and there he has found that the trouble with most of these plays that deal with religion in one form or another is that their authors, in turn, have not sufficiently criticized them. What Hurlbut has seen is a long succession of dramas in which the heroine, fired by the holy teachings of the handsome hero, follows him into the Garden of Allah, there presumably to spend the soft, moonlit nights entirely in prayer; in which a passionate young woman who has spent her life with a crippled octogenarian atheist is uplifted only spiritually by a young clergyman bearing a striking resemblance to James J. Corbett; and wherein a harlot, played by a very lovely and very young blonde actress, is won from her evil ways by the devout faith of a man of God whose wife has a face that would rout the Anti-Saloon League. Beholding this ingenuous dramatic nonsense, Mr. Hurlbut has let out an obscene laugh, has retired to his studio, and has written a criticism of it.

What Hurlbut has actually done, of course, is simply to dig up the venerable platitude on the close relation of sexual and religious hysteria and to incorporate it into one of these familiar piffle-puffs. If he were a novelist and were to have done the same thing he would, obviously enough, have attracted no attention. But as the stage is ever the grazing-ground of banalities and as the theatre generally gets excited over something that is an old story everywhere else, he has been hailed as a fellow of mentality and something of a doctor-professor in the way of the new psychology. What he is, rather, as must be plain, is merely a clever fellow who has contrived to make holding an intrinsically crude piece of dramatic writing by converting it into a commentary on the plots of numerous plays that have dealt with the same subject. Every once in a while a play that similarly comments on other plays in its own category creates a like stir. In such cases, it is not the play so much as the ironic criticism with which the play is embellished that induces the prosperous gabble.

The reaction is readily intelligible. After years of religious plays in which the theme has been approached in sentimental terms, the theatre audience is ready to hail enthusiastically a right-about-face, as it is always ready to hail a turtle-turn of theme in any dramatic direction. It has been thus that the first crook play to make the crook a hero instead of the stenciled villain has been successful, and it is thus that the first play to make the seduced girl decline to marry her seducer has created a prodigious flutter. Merit has very little to do with the favor with which such plays are received; it is simply the novelty of them that fetches the yokels. This yearning for novelty, which has existed in one form or another ever since the theatre began, was responsible, some years back, for the wave of plays with trick endings. Playwrights ran out of ways to make their familiar themes novel, so in their quandary hit upon the device of tricking the popular audience into imagining they had made the themes novel by tacking on codas in which they either stated that the stale manner in which they had handled the familiar themes was a deliberate joke at the audience's expense, or that the antiquated play the audience had just seen was a story being related by a grandfather to his grandchild. Hurlbut

196

has not gone in for a trick ending; what he has negotiated is simply what may be called a trick middle. Just as his play is beginning, along toward ten o'clock, to be familiar to his audience, he enters it with a treatise on phallic symbolism. At ten minutes after ten, the brief lecture over, his play proceeds again duly on its recognizable course, but the audience has been adroitly fooled —startled is perhaps the better word—into imagining that what follows the little lecture is very new stuff, and the play accordingly prospers out of the auditorium self-befuddlement.

Mr. Hurlbut's technique is, patently, anything but new. There are scores of instances where shrewd playmakers have resorted to the same stratagem. The present playwright's success is due to the circumstance that his trick middle is of a theatrically scandalous nature. Stanley Houghton's "Hindle Wakes" was successful in arousing interest for the same reason; so was Sidney Howard's "They Knew What They Wanted"; so have been any number of plays in the last fifteen years. While not always an arbitrary device, while not always contrived and executed with one eye on the box-office, the tactic more often is just that. The playwright who practises the dodge is pretty generally found to be a fellow set chiefly upon startling the dollars out of the trade's pockets.

§ 13

It is unfortunate that Mr. Galsworthy should elect the play, "Escape," as his swan song to the theatre. A dramatic career as distinguished as his has been deserves a better ending. To wind it up with this play is much as if Shaw had trusted to "Press Cuttings" for his final blaze of glory, or Hauptmann to "Die Jungfern von Bischofsberg." While I do not mean, plainly enough, to place Galsworthy in the high company of the aforementioned dramatists, his position in the contemporary theatre has been sufficiently important to merit a sounder adieu than this. For "Escape" must rank with such of his works as "The Fugitive," "A Bit o' Love," "Windows," "The Skin Game" and the like as one of his feeblest enterprises. One cannot help believing that its reception in certain quarters as a meritorious job must be attributed to the critical philosophy set forth by one of the critics in

198

"Fanny's First Play": that if a play be signed with the name of a good author, it is a good play, and if it be signed with the name of a bad one, it is a bad play.

"Escape," though it bears the name of a good dramatist, is none the less a bad play. Its creator has imagined an excellent theme—the reactions to the predicament of an escaped convict on the part of a diversity of his fellow countrymen—and has done little more with it than to permit it to be commented upon by a series of flapper intelligences. At only one point in the play, in the very last scene, does he bring his theme face to face with a relatively critical mind and a critical philosophic situation, and then all he has to offer is the bewhiskered speculation, favorite of a whole library of second-rate sentimental fiction, as to what Christ would have done in a like juncture. The body of the drama is taken up with the attitudes toward the escaped convict of an undeviating procession of soft-heads: a susceptible ingénue, a child who collects autographs, a sweet one in blue pajamas and a pink négligé, a young woman who sentimentalizes the hunting of foxes, an addle-pated fat wench who enjoys roadside picnicking, a hotel chamber-maid, a doddering old man, a couple of jail-wardens given to a high delight in the moving pictures, a silly-ass musical comedy Englishman stepped straight out of the comic weeklies, a village constable, a yokel, and a couple of stone-cutters. It is through such instruments that Galsworthy filters his theme, bringing into conflict with it upon no single occasion anything approaching a real mind or an experienced emotion. The one trivial exception is to be had in the case of the clergyman in the final episode and there, as I have observed, Galsworthy merely continues his complete surrender to sentimentality.

"Escape" belongs to the catalogue of Galsworthy's valentine drama, along with "A Bit o' Love" and similar plays. Sentimentality is thick upon it, like steam in a candy kitchen, and obscures any values that the drama might have possessed. I may exaggerate somewhat when I say that the impression that one gains from it is much like the one induced by the old Hanlon tinsel shows, in which the hero, a handsome fellow in purple tights in quest of the elusive blonde prima donna, passed through a dozen scene-changes beset variously by acrobats dressed as devils, contraltos in the robes of witches and contortionists with sinister eyes painted in the middle of their fore-heads, but I believe that I do not exaggerate too greatly. The conflicts that Galsworthy interposes in the path of his migratory hero are largely of a piece with those of these old extravaganzas. Were so much as a single character from one of Shaw's plays—or even one of Brieux's—to wander into the text for a moment and deliver a few remarks on the subject in hand, the play would promptly take on a sliver of the conviction it lacks, for then at least one or two of the sensible questions that presently rattle rebelliously, insistently and im-patiently in the audience's head might be posed and so momentarily dissipate the all-enveloping sentimental fog. As the play stands, all that the author does is to ask sociological questions of the kindergarten class. In addition to the dubious thematic handling, Galsworthy has never written poorer drama. Such an episode as that dealing with the two wardens waiting to capture the convict on the dark moor, with its jokes about Charlie Chaplin and Duggie Fairbanks and its slapstick finale with the cops rolling around on the ground in each other's arms, constitutes a revue skit of the cheapest sort. Nor are such jejune observations as the street-walker's "Clean streets!—that's the cry. Clean *men!* That'd be better!", such dramatic devices as the whistling of a popular music show tune by way of signal, and such jocosities as concern painful corns entirely what one has a right to expect from a man of Mr. Galsworthy's eminence.

Mr. Galsworthy's eminence? To what, looking back upon his long and honorable career as a dramatist, has that eminence been due? It is the custom to answer that it is and has been due to certain qualities of mind, an intelligence at once calm and discerning, and one expert in surveying both sides of a question and meditating more or less profoundly the tilting of the scales now this way and now that. But I doubt it. The eminence of Mr. Galsworthy in the field of drama is and has been due to the dignity not of his thought, but to the dignity of his emotions. One can name a number of dramatists with minds on a level with Galsworthy's who have not achieved anything like his eminence, for they have not, like him, possessed synchronously the emotions of scholars and gentlemen. The true mark of an artist is to be found not in his head, but in his heart, or at least in what passes for the seat and capital of his emotions. Many a playwright with a clear head has had muddy emotions, and many a playwright with a soundly reasoning mind has found it corrupted, in dramatic practice, by cheap feeling. Galsworthy's emotions are those of a civilized gentleman. The emotions of so many of the younger British playwrights of the day are those of wise and sophisticated, and very clever, bounders. It is, to conclude, therefore a great pity that so worthy an exponent of the modern drama should say goodbye to it with so puny and discreditable an example of the art he has dignified and adorned.

THE QUESTION OF PASSIONS

The conventional criticism of any such play as, for example, Rosso di San Secondo's "Marionette, che Passione!" is that the emotions and perturbations of its characters are too alien either to persuade or interest the Anglo-Saxon spectator. It is a criticism that we hear whenever one of the more intensely amorous dramas of the Latin countries comes our way, and it is a criticism that, for sheer sophistry, one must go a long distance to equal. That the Anglo-Saxon cardiac psychology is somewhat different from that of the Latin needs no arguing, but that this difference makes the Anglo-Saxon unresponsive to plays emphasizing it calls for a great deal. The criticism is merely a convenient cloak under which its expounders conceal their inability to get at the core of the matter.

It is not the passions of the Latin drama that seem unreal and indeed often mutinously humorous to the Anglo-Saxon audience, but the Anglo-

Saxon actors who are put forth to affect them. The case is different, as everyone knows, when an Italian or Spanish or French drama of the species under discussion is played in an Anglo-Saxon community by Italian, Spanish or French actors. One hears no snickers then, save from persons who do not understand the language and to whom the drama accordingly and as a matter of course takes on the air of a somewhat comical moving picture. But when the drama is translated into English and the passions of its Pietros, Gonzalos and Raouls are put into the mouths and antics of Piccadilly and Broadway actors, they quite naturally strike the spectator not only as alien but as extremely jocose. I am speaking, of course, of the modern drama, for once you put actors into costume and relegate their activities to a past period, an audience is ready to grant anything, bad acting in particular, and to enjoy it. But when you show an English or American audience a painfully obvious English or American actor in a Hawes and Curtis suit and a sanitary-barbershop hair-cut who is put down in the program as Don Basilio Ramón Gumersindo Contreras and who, after calling upon his ancestor, Solórzano y Pereira Mendoza, to bear witness to the outraged family honor, pulls out a Sixteenth Century stiletto and stabs himself through the liver because his sister has married a peon—well, I ask you.

The majority of the kind of plays I am alluding to are produced in just this way. The translations are often good enough, the *décor* is often sufficiently apposite and the producer generally goes so far toward verisimilitude as to hire a real Italian or Frenchman to play the part of the waiter in the private supper-room scene, but the actors who are disclosed in the important rôles are uniformly by nature, temperament and physical appearance about as aptly suited to them as a company of Italian, Spanish or French actors would be to "Is Zat So?" or "Porgy." The argument here, of course, is that competent English or American actors should be able so to alter their actual personalities as realistically to suggest the nature and deportment of the alien characters entrusted to them, but an argument, however convincing, is one thing and established fact is another. And the established fact, with so few exceptions that they may be dismissed, is that when English or American actors try to make persuasive the passions of D'Annunzio, Guiméra or Porto-Riche they almost always succeed only in making their audiences laugh. If there is another reason for the failure of an Anglo-Saxon audience to react satisfactorily to the stranger emotions of an alien drama, I am at a loss to account for it. Surely no one would be so foolish as to contend that Anglo-Saxons are as generally unresponsive to so-called alien passions when they are set forth in translated modern novels; the success of any number of such novels in England and America, from those of Anatole France to those of Blasco Ibáñez, is ample proof of the emotional receptivity of Anglo-Saxons when no disconcerting barriers are put in the way. Surely, too, no one would think for a moment of arguing that an Anglo-Saxon audience is unresponsive to the unusual passions of much of the classic drama. And, to go even farther, we may convince ourselves that, when it comes to these theoretically alien and unfamiliar emotional disturbances, we have considerable evidence from the daily newspapers—not counting the tabloids—that Italian, Spanish and French passions

are in as full operation on the part, say, of New
York and Chicago Americans as they are in their
native lands. It is not the alien passions, but the
alien funnels of those passions, that generate the
Anglo-Saxon titters. When an audience sees Mr.
Frank Morgan, for example, a man as completely
suggestive of Broadway as *Variety*, pretending,
without make-up, in the San Secondo opus, that
he is a passionate Italian, conducting himself like a
libretto by Leoncavallo and drinking a glass of
poisoned champagne because his fair one has gone
to the Italian equivalent of Atlantic City with a
rival, it is readily to be forgiven for echoing the
sentiment of a certain illustrious, if deplorably
vulgar, predecessor of *Kriegsherr* Foch.

THEATRICALIZED THEATRE

A few years ago there appeared an article in the Italian periodical, *Le Futurisme*, by one Marinetti, of Milan, urging against the present-day theatre the fact that it lacks all bounce and gaiety. Not the stage of the theatre, which now and then discloses something to lift the miserable human psyche into the celestial regions of amusement, but the theatre itself, which seldom discloses anything of the kind. The theatre itself, the writer pointed out, is generally a dark, damp, forbidding house, as unsuggestive, physically, of gaiety as a Milanese *scuderìa*. What it needs is something to convert it from its present austere and chilled condition into a place that wears at least a string of bright beads and a few vine leaves in its hair. What it needs, in short, is less of a show on the stage and more of a show in the auditorium, since the theatre of today is actually only one-fourth theatre (that part of it that is the stage) and three-fourths (or the rest of it) cold, hard, uninviting chairs surrounded by bleak walls that make it indistinguishable from an undertaking parlor, minus only the latter's cheerful flowers and stimulating organ.

There are, of course, occasions when the theatre is properly of such an austere mien, say, when fine dramatic art occupies its stage. But for one such occasion there are a hundred when an austere air is no more suited to it than it would be to a hot-dog stand. In the theatre as we engage it in the world today, we find that a particular playhouse often discloses a platform that, in a single season, is held successively by tragedy, comedy, melodrama, pantomime, farce, musical comedy and what not. There are exceptions, to be sure; there are certain theatres that resolutely dedicate their stages to a specific form of drama; but, in the main, one encounters stages that, as units, are given over indiscriminately to Shakespeare one day and Mephistophelian-looking gentlemen who make bowls of goldfish disappear the next, to problem dramas one week and the next to Hindu gentlemen who can have pins stuck into their epidermises without feeling them, and to "Iphigenia at Aulis" one month

210

and to a colored song and dance show the month after. Surely, a theatre that houses a farce in which a fat man hides under the bed to avoid the ingénue's irate Uncle Adolph should look and actually be a bit different from a theatre that houses a tragedy in which all the leading characters have inherited lewd spirochætæ and blow their brains out. It caters to people in an entirely different mood; but, though it caters to such people, it fails to cater to that mood. The Comédie Française or the Deutsches-Theater or the Hampden .in New York are all right as they are; their physical atmosphere is appropriate to their stage traffic. But the majority of theatres to the left and right of them in their respective cities and similar theatres in Vienna, Madrid, Rome, London and Chicago four times out of every five no more satisfactorily reflect their proper natures than so many profusely fly-specked mirrors. Thus, today, seeing "John Gabriel Borkman" in a theatre where, only the week before, one has seen a music show is much like asking one to listen to "Vom Tode" in a night-club, and expecting one to enjoy it.

Discussing specifically the subject of vaudeville

theatres, the Italian writer pointed out the complete absurdity of playhouses resembling in every detail dramatic theatres yet offering to their audiences such violently discrepant and utterly discordant things as trained geese, red-nosed comedians in green pants, soft-shoe dancers and virtuosi of the banjo. Such theatres most assuredly should mirror their stages and should themselves inculcate in their audiences at least a measure of the mood which the platform didos were designed and seek to inculcate. It was the writer's suggestion, for example, that the vaudeville auditorium chairs should be of the trick variety, that at intervals the ushers should sneak up behind the fat, bald-headed men in the audience and tickle their pates with feathers, that as the older and more sedate ladies of the audience entered the door they should have "Please kick me" signs stuck onto their bustles, and that the house should be sprayed along toward the middle of the performance with some kind of powder that would make everybody sneeze. These may not be exactly our Italian friend's suggestions —my memory is not too accurate on the point— but they hint at the general contour of his recommendations. Exaggerated though they are, they indicate to a degree just what is lacking in the vaudeville dumps and what, by virtue of this lack, is gradually putting the vaudeville business in limbo. Go into any first-class American vaudeville theatre today and you will catch sight of a house full of faces that, whatever the nature of the stage performance, are in the main as long and sour as the faces at a performance of "The Cenci." It is only along toward 10:15, if the bill be a sufficiently amusing one, that the management succeeds in making the audience melt even partly and give way to its funny-bone. The theatre itself has stood in the way in the meantime; it has taken the audience the intervening hours to surmount and conquer the heavy mood which the playhouse has superimposed upon it.

The changes that certain revue and music show producers have made in their theatres in recent years, together with the devices that have been exercised by various purveyors of other forms of light entertainment, show clearly that our impresarios are beginning to be aware of the truth of the new theatre theory. The runway, installed in revue houses, to bring gaiety from behind the footlights into the midst of the audience; the broad stage aprons whereon dancers and clowns cavort in close proximity to the customers; the use of the aisles for chorus numbers; the monkeyshines of "plants" in the boxes; the gorillas that run up and down the aisles pursued by a dozen actors dressed as policemen; the distribution of "plants" among the audience to give the latter the feeling of sharing in the stage traffic; such things as illuminated auditorium side-walls and cages of canaries which Reinhardt put into his Berlin Kammerspiele; such theatres as the Redoutensaal of Vienna; such tricks as smelling up the house with various kinds of perfume, a device of music show producers to "get over" their flower songs; the use of incense in Oriental plays, the fumes of which spread over the auditorium; the chorus custom of playing ball with the members of the audience and of entering into similar intimate amusement relations with the trade in the seats—all such things are an indication that something has long been lacking in the theatres themselves and that the lack is being gradually appreciated. In due time, it will be rectified completely. And the moment it is thus rectified we shall see the dawn of a newly prosperous theatrical day. The French saw the need, in part, years ago and their music halls, at least, have been converted into physically relevant and appropriate houses.

But there are theatres other than revue houses that call for a change. A theatre in which a loud, low farce, for instance, is being played should be a theatre that itself has something of the loud, low farce's spirit. As a usual thing, at least in America, however, it no more cultivates the farcical spirit in its sitters than a dentist's chair cultivates the spirit of romance. What is needed on such occasions is a house that imparts a sense of fun the moment one enters it. The ticket-taker should be dressed up as a "What-Is-It?" and should trip up each patron as he crosses the threshold, the house-manager should stand in the lobby and pass out loaded cigars, the ushers should wear sleigh-bells and the programs should be on long rubber bands which would cause them to snap back out of the customers' hands, the backs of the chairs should have trick mirrors on them, the chairs themselves should every once in a while collapse and land their occupants on the floor, the gallery patrons should be supplied with confetti, there should be toy balloons for the butter and egg men and their sweet ones, the candy on sale in the rear aisle should be filled with red pepper, the stairs leading to the smoking-room and ladies' parlor should be collapsible, the arms of the chairs should be connected with an electric current which should be turned on at appropriate moments during the course of the evening, and everyone should, upon entering the theatre, be given a colored paper hat, a set of false whiskers, a pair of cardboard ears, a boutonnière that squirts water, a few rotten tomatoes, and a tack to place on his neighbor's seat. And what is true of the farce theatre is true of the melodrama theatre and each of the other relatively unimportant yet presently absurdly dignified and overly serious theatres. Each of these should, in its different way, be treated as treatment has been suggested for the farce *Lusthaus*. For example, the mystery melodrama theatre should have a bizarre and spooky illumination, the ushers should be dressed as ghosts or burglars and should shoot off pistols as they show the patrons to their seats, the

216

lavatory should be entered through a sliding panel, there should be secretly manipulated trap-doors under the seats through which the patrons' hats might periodically be made to disappear from under their chairs and then again to reappear, the box-office attendants should wear black masks, sudden terrifying screams should issue during the entr'actes from the ladies' room, and Mr. William Lyon Phelps should be mysteriously kidnapped by the house-manager sometime during the first act.

As I have said, one of these days our managers will wake up to the situation and theatregoing will then become almost as much of a sport and pleasure as bull-fighting or lynching. For let these managers remember, if they believe that I am given to deplorable levity, that the auditorium show, in the broadest and best sense of the world, was not above the Greeks in their heyday nor above the playwriting and managerial genius of a fellow named Shakespeare.

THE TRIVIAL PLAY

If, from time to time in the course of my critical activities, I select for discussion trivial plays which reach the storehouse before the words on them reach my readers, it is because now and then I find in them certain elements that suggest the bases for general critical doctrines. The perfect play, after all, offers small ground for interesting critical exploration. One may write of it extensively; one may even write of it entertainingly, provided one exercise a care that one's commentary concern itself with a half-dozen or more sprightly subjects only indirectly associated with the matter in hand; one may praise, praise and praise yet again. But, after the fireworks are over, there is found to be little new in the way of contribution to critical knowledge, for all the things that may be said of perfect plays have already been said a hundred times and said better than anyone presently performing in the critical pulpit, myself surely included, can say them. Not one thing written of the drama of Shakespeare in the last twenty years, for instance, contains anything seriously to interest the student who knows the Shakespearian criticism of earlier years. And nothing has been said of the finest work produced in our time that hasn't been a mere cuckooing of what was written of the finest work of other times by the critics of other days.

The objection to this point of view is naturally the obvious one of protesting that, if it be valid, all criticism must henceforth concern itself chiefly with relatively inferior works. The objection is silly. The point is simply that, since we know what absolute worth is and since only the veriest num-skulls among critics, due to their own shortcom-ings, protest the contrary, the business of criticism has become the business not so much of arguing that what is excellent is excellent as of arguing that what is not excellent should be excellent, and trying to indicate, as best it can, the ways and means gradually to make it so. Criticism, otherwise, is of small service and is converted into a mere parlor game of slap-hands, giving issue only to an automatic applause that turns the true artist's stomach. The critic who consistently devotes himself to announcing that what is good is good is in the position of the clergyman who consistently devotes himself to announcing the goodness of God, and in the process bores his congregation, already presumably privy to the news, to death.

Read the criticisms of the classics written in the last two decades and try to find one thing new in them. One thing new, that is, of critical value. You will find a number of critical estimates that present the stale facts in a fresh manner; you will even find some, like certain of my own, if you will forgive me the presumption, that seem to have a measure of new and vital bounce; but if you will look closely into any of these, my own in particular, you will discover to your chagrin that there is not a blessed new idea in them from nose to tail and that what you mistook for new ideas were simply so many tricks of the scrivening art. It is very easy to lay hold of an idea so old that its beard trails the dust and make it seem as frisky as a colt with turpentine up it, if one knows the persuading chicanery of the English language. And it is equally easy, by the exercise of crafty literary hocus-

pocus, to convince the majority of readers. For it
is a Polichinelle secret, known surely to men whose
trade is the merchanting of opinions, that—contrary to the general belief in certain bemused
quarters—a reader wishes above all things to be
convinced by his writer. And not only does he wish
to be convinced; he actually lends to the writer a
volitional self-hypnosis. I speak, of course, not of
the occasional mountebank who reads criticism
only for the satisfaction he may get from loudly
disputing it, whether he believes it to be right or
not, but of the average, quiet, intelligent and open-
minded man who is seriously interested in the subject. Such a man does not seek substantiation of
his own beliefs so much as he seeks the critic's substantiation of the latter's own beliefs. Otherwise,
why the tremendous popularity of the critical writings of Shaw and others who have taken the *contra
mundum* attitude and, by the exercise of wily
thinking and writing, given it an apparently substantial foundation of plausibility? The reader of
Shaw, as the reader of Nietzsche before him and as
the reader of Voltaire before *him,* comes to market
not to refuse to buy, but to buy and fetch back

home. A man with a sore throat does not go to a doctor to be told that he hasn't a sore throat; he knows damned well that he has a sore throat and he wants to get rid of it. In the same way, a man does not go to a critic to be told that his opinions are well; he goes to be told that many of them are sick, and what the cure is. The critic who simply echoes the opinions of his readers is either a sad newspaper dolt on a sadder newspaper, or one whose publisher loses money if he prints more than five hundred copies of his book. I am not saying —it should be plain—that the critic who arbitrarily postures an oppugnant point of view, and without the justification of a sound and workmanlike knowledge, can win his reader as he would for long, even where the reader is a more or less willing victim. What I am saying is rather that the reader does not wish to go on hearing the same old argument that one and one make two, advanced by a mathematician who doesn't know what two and two make, so much as he longs, and understandably, to hear from someone gifted in the art of subtraction as well as multiplication that one minus one—the former digit being platitude and the latter being common-sense—leaves nothing.

Many of the most valuable contributions to dramatic criticism have been inspired by negligible dramatic and poetical works; many of the least valuable by modern critics who, laboring under the delusion of professional dignity, have sought to plough up already long ploughed-up classical ground. Thus, in the former category, we have a share of the critical wisdom of D'Aubignac taking flower from such things as the "Esther" of Du Ryer; of John Dennis from trivial comedies that passed quickly into limbo; of Dryden from the "Rollo" of the Messrs. Fletcher, Rowley and Massinger, to say nothing of the very worst of Ben Jonson; of Thomas Rymer from Buckingham's "The Rehearsal"; of Addison from Otway's "The Orphan"; of Goethe from Raupach's "Erdennacht," Klopstock's "Hermann's Schlacht" and the like; of the younger Dumas from the worst of Scribe; of Brunetière from the collaborations of Paul Bocage and Octave Feuillet; of Schlegel from the *pièces à tiroir* of Boursault and the hollowness of Gottsched; of Coleridge from negligible German tragedies; of Hazlitt from such things as Mrs. Centlivre confected, to say nothing of Gay's "What-d'ye-call-it?", Cibber's mediocrities and the plays of Bickerstaff, Mrs. Cowley, Murphy and company; and, to come closer to the moment, of Shaw from the unspeakable trash produced in the London theatres in the 1890's. . . . As for the other side of the critical picture, I need only refer the skeptic to any four out of five present-day professorial tomes that he will find at the nearest bookstall.

Some such completely negligible and trivial play as Mr. Knowles Entrikin's "Seed of the Brute," for example, causes one to reflect upon the great distance that often intervenes between what is merely truthful theatre and what is truthful life. At certain of its points, this play has the false ring of truth that succeeds in impressing such persons as are readily deceived by a dexterous manipulation of the devices of the theatre, but at no point does its veneer of theatrical truth merge plausibly with worldly verisimilitude. Its aim is realism; its achievement is simply stage realism. It gets no closer to actuality than a horse race in a Drury Lane melodrama; the sound of the dramatic tread-mill and the glycerine that passes for perspiration are always discernible. Yet such is the confusion in real values by the present-day audience that falsity persuasively presented often—at least for a time—makes a deeper impression and registers a deeper conviction than stark reality not trickily theatricalized.

The one great defect in the equipment of the majority of the younger playwrights currently working in the Anglo-American theatre is the be-lief, and the assiduous practice of it, that to make truth seem truthful in the theatre it is necessary first to filter it through the dubious hypocausts and shell-games of dramaturgy. What results is almost uniformly truth rid of all truth: truth so exag-gerated as to be no more itself than the reflection of a man in a trick mirror is a reflection of him-self. This result, as the reflection in the trick mirror, is sometimes startling and often amusing, but it is at the same time plainly ridiculous. A dramatist like Hauptmann, in a play like "The Weavers," appreciating that true realism is, after all, but poetry without a shave, contrives an enormous effect by laying hold of truth and letting it find its way to the stage through the fancy of an artist rather than through the prestidigitation of a dramatist. A dramatist like Gorki, in "Nachtasyl," does the same. For such men know that all this talk of the necessary exaggeration of truth and realism in the theatre is nonsensical, and that the theatre simply takes life and the truth off their stilts and reduces them to pigmies that antic on a platform for a couple of hours and leave, perhaps, behind them a hint of that greater drama that is the world. Lesser men, and more vainglorious ones, seek to intensify life, and what they produce, accordingly, is merely cheap showshop melodrama.

Some of the poorest plays known to us are truthful theatre; that is, plays which, by an artful employment of proscenium dodges, are made to seem plausible to the average person during the two hours he sits before them. George Kelly's "Daisy Mayme," though it has some reportorial virtues, is such a play. It takes truth and so smears up its face with grease-paint (though the smearing is deftly enough managed) that, when it is over, one has the impression of having looked out of a window onto life but, unfortunately, at a moment when a circus parade was passing. For there is occasionally grease-paint in actual life too; looking out upon the world we as often see an organ grinder's monkey or a Knights of Pythias conclave as we see a starving beggar or a mother burying her baby son. So many of our playwrights, in gazing out of the window, see the former and imagine that, because it adorns the sunlight of actuality, it is necessarily part and parcel of living, human truth. Thus we behold the countless Noël Cowards and Dion Titheradges and Shipmans and Willard Macks going down into the street to find humanity and fetching back up with them into the theatre little more than stray clowns out of one-ring circuses, sandwich men with false moustaches and policewomen disguised as honest street-walkers.

If plays that are truthful chiefly in terms of the theatre are so often bad plays, plays that are of so ingrained, uncompromising and unadorned a truth that they fail in the Anglo-American theatre are not less often found to be of proportionate merit. In this catalogue, we have plays like Brieux's "Les

Hannetons," Schönherr's "Kindertragödie" and, perhaps more legitimately to name plays whose content is closer to the native sympathy and comprehension, such lesser exhibits as the Howard-Mizner "The Only Law," Maugham's "Our Betters" and Rita Wellman's "The Gentile Wife." Plays like these put the truth out close to the footlights and let it stand there disconcertingly while the dramatist is giving the necessary three-dollar show back of it, where plays of the other sort put the truth in the background and distract the audience's attention from it with the show going on down front. In the former plays, the play is secondary to the truth; in the latter, the truth is secondary to the play. The one dramatizes the truth; the other theatricalizes it—and between the two, all playing with words aside, there is the difference between the truth as we see it with our own eyes and the truth as we hear it somewhat dubiously related by a stranger.

Some such triviality as Mr. Robert McLaughlin's "The Pearl of Great Price" brings us to reflect, in turn, upon the dramatic importance that the Anglo-American public in the aggregate still attaches to female chastity. While the French, the Italians, the Germans, the Austrians and the Hungarians got over this theatrical emotional disease some time ago, the Anglo-American continues gladly to pay out his hard-earned money and to waste valuable hours in return for the gratification of (*1*) being assured that woman's virtue is her greatest jewel and (*2*) being shown the overthrow of such baleful forces as playwrights present in the light of gem collectors. Although the Anglo-American takes pride in his increasing liberality in the matter of dramatic themes, the fact remains that that liberality is confined to a relatively small element and that modern drama which departs from the pure heroine, while it now and again enjoys a very considerable prosperity in London or New York, almost always comes a cropper in the more representative and typical towns and cities of the interior of either country. What is more, even in those instances where the peccable heroine enjoys a metropolitan box-office prosperity, we find that a sop is still often necessary in the form of a tragic end for the poor girl or of the embodiment of the rôle by an actress already so popular and beloved of audiences that the unpopularity of the character she plays is partly lost sight of. To test the Anglo-American attitude, all one need do is to regard the nature of the moving pictures that make millions of dollars catering to it. The pictures made in Germany and in France often indicate a completely different point of view on the part of the peoples of those countries, whereas those manufactured in America and in England demonstrate that female virtue is still the great box-office card that it was fifty years ago. To argue that censorship in England and America prevents the public from adopting another attitude is simply foolish. Facts are facts, and the facts are that the publics of these countries relish the pure movie drivel to the extent of making it a gold-mine for the producers. These producers should be grateful to the censors for keeping a sufficient number of their films biologically sacrosanct, for if it were not for the censors they would very probably lose their shirts. The exceptional cases where plays exhibiting unapologetic, unchaste heroines have made money in the general Anglo-American theatre during the last twenty years may be counted on the fingers of the hands. For every such play there have been a dozen flying the flag of female virtue that have been prosperous. Try to arrive at similar comparative statistics in France, Germany, Austria, Hungary or Italy and you'll have a time of it!

This "Pearl of Great Price" is, like "Everywoman" and "Experience," a modernization of the ancient morality play, and is dreadful flapdoodle. Yet in the criticism of these modern versions of the old moralities I have a feeling that one important point is regularly and conveniently overlooked, and that is that the Sixteenth Century morality plays were almost as bad as these present-day versions that everyone makes fun of. "Everyman," "The Trial of Pleasure," "All For Money," "The Three Ladies of London," "Un Empereur Qui Tua Son Neveu," "La Tragédie Française," "The World and the Child," "The Nature of the Four Elements," "Wit and Science," "Albion Knight"—from first to last, the art of the drama reduced to the art of the kindergarten. Save for their historical significance, such plays are worth no more consideration than their modern paraphrases. All are worthless.

CHRONICLE OF VICES AND CRIMES

§ 1

The defective education and consequent minimum of taste in the instance of the great masses of Americans has resulted, naturally enough, in the substitution of a veneration of tricks as against sound and honest artistic performance. A man who plays the violin standing on his head thus gets five times more applause than a competent musician standing on his feet. A man who paints a bad picture of a pretty woman is thus estimated above the man who paints a good picture of a homely one. And a man who writes a novel full of surprising twists and turns of plot is thus valued above one who writes a profound, if less lively, study of character.

§ 2

The will to think is perhaps the greatest of the handicaps that beset our young gentlemen of the theatre. There are among these young fellows some who show a measure of talent for the writing of interesting and diverting stage pieces, but who spoil that talent by believing it to be necessary for them to constitute themselves philosophers as well. Every now and then a play comes along that, if left alone by its author, would be entertaining stuff, but that has been made a dreadful bore by the injection into it of quasi-profundities on the social, economic and other ills of the day. With one or two exceptions, the American drama is best when it deals simply either with straight emotion or straight humor. In such cases we periodically get from it plays of considerable merit. But, almost without exception, when the American drama tries to think it becomes ridiculous. This is doubtless due to the fact that the theatre here seems not to exercise much appeal to the better minds among either our oldsters or younger men and attracts chiefly an inferior grade of intelligence. In England, where men like Shaw and Galsworthy are drawn to it; in France, where the best minds are and always have been deeply interested in it; in Germany, where it attracts men like Hauptmann, and in Italy, where it attracts such as Pirandello, the situation is different. But in America the theatre is looked down upon by men of any intellect—to their discredit and perhaps as a mark of an intrinsically bourgeois civilization—and the writing of its plays is left, accordingly, to what may be described as the knee-pants intelligentsia.

It is a characteristic of the young playwright that he wishes, in a single play, to say everything that is in his mind, where the adult and wiser playwright knows that good plays are to be written only by forgetting almost everything that is in his mind. The young man writes his play not content with making it an amusing play but insists also upon making it an important one. His notion of such importance usually lies in interrupting his otherwise entertaining play every now and again with dank speeches in the manner of undergraduate theses generalizing upon the actions of his specific characters and essaying to give them a cosmic significance. Thus, just as an audience is beginning to be amused by the spectacle of a young woman chasing a truck-driver around the drawing-room in an attempt at seduction, the young Sardou calls a halt and makes the truck-driver stop short in his tracks and deliver a Shavian monologue deploring the new morality. This, of course, passes for sincerity and thinking on the part of our young men and leads them to believe that, in addition to the satisfaction of the royalities, they will be praised by the more astute critics for trying to do something above the average and improving the condition of the native drama. Yet the young men actually do nothing but make fools of themselves, for while it does not take genius to write amusing shows, it does take genius to wear becomingly the whiskers of metaphysics.

§ 3

One generally finds that the more authentic contributions to the art of drama are unequivocally much less ennobling, as the word goes, than the inferior ones. Thus, "Goat Song," Franz Werfel's estimable play, does nothing more than to depress man with the philosophy that the monstrous seed of revolution with its trail of devastation will never die from the world, while such a piece of balderdash as "The Love City," by a fellow countryman of Werfel's, inspirits him with the philosophy that the forces of evil must inevitably meet with defeat. Thus again, "The Great God Brown," Eugene O'Neill's beautifully imaginative work, bears in upon man's consciousness the rueful facts that hypocrisy triumphs in this world where truth and forthrightness fail, that noble dreams must go down to defeat before the world's prosaicism, that what the world demands is mere show and pretence, and that heartache and desolation are ever the reward of great, deep and faithful love—where, on the other hand, "The Shanghai Gesture," a *pâté* of box-office drivel, sends the spectator home with the comforting conviction that earthly lust resolves itself into tragedy, that the sinner must soon or late pay a grievous penalty and that vice is ever less profitable than virtue. Thus further, Ibsen's "Little Eyolf," aiming to be a sermon against selfishness, actually makes mankind bitterly despairful with its demonstration that egoism, which is mortal man's one pragmatic religion and his one potential victorious battle-cry, is the faith of the humiliated and defeated; "Hedda Gabler" instils a sense of

236

the utter futility of life by showing that the bad angel of man's destiny holds ever the whip-hand; and "John Gabriel Borkman" puts hope and trust to rout with its doctrine of the eternal cruel indifference and selfishness of one's offspring and with its categorical enunciation of age's chagrin and suffering. Such an unmitigated gimcrack as Capek's "The Makropoulos Secret," on the contrary, gladdens the mortal soul with the thesis that the short span of life allotted to man by God is infinitely more desirable than a longer span would be; such a tenth-rate French boulevard play as Fauchois' "The Monkey Talks" warms the human heart and mind with a promulgation of the tenet that man's outward self, however ugly, has beneath it a true radiance and that the reward of honest love is a permanent happiness; and such commercial exhibits as "Love 'Em and Leave 'Em" and "Puppy Love" bring God nearer to earth with the eloquent assurance that self-sacrifice is the most exalted of human acts and that true affection will irresistibly find a way to the human heart.

§ 4

The generality of young English playwrights of the present time take adultery so seriously while their actors take it so lightly. As men, they view *crim. con.* with the eyes of so many pastors but as playwrights, in shamefaced effort to hide their true attitude and by way of persuading the world at large that they are very blasé and sophisticated fellows, they make a show of viewing it as so many *dégagé* rakes. They are clearly moralists in their own consciences and superficially worldly *raisonneurs* in their stage exhibits. They make an elaborate pretence of Galllic casualness, but it is very easy to read between the lines and discern there the conventional Anglo-Saxon. One gets the impression, on the whole, of evangelists disguised as college boys cutting up in a geisha house. A further characteristic of these playwrights is the attempt to extract important emotions from trivial people. Their characters are weaklings, mentally and emotionally, and they would have us interested in giants. The effect is much the same as viewing a

238

lot of undersized nincompoops who happen to have curls on their foreheads and nice little bellies and who hence imagine themselves to be and conduct themselves as Napoleons. In their aim to be smartly indifferent to the usual alarms of the sex world their plays succeed only in being transparently and bumptiously egregious, like a man who picks up the oyster fork for his soup and who, for all the raised eyebrows, goes blandly on, with a fine show of self-assurance, using it.

§ 5

One would think that, with the endless production of so-called mystery plays, the public would have had its fill of them and would begin to tire of this form of theatrical diversion. This, particularly, as the various other forms of analogous entertainment, such as prestidigitators, vaudeville mind-readers, cross-word puzzles and the like seem to have lost their erstwhile hold upon the public. Yet what one would think is doubtless wrong, for of all the species of theatrical amusement the mystery play has held out the longest in popular esteem. For fifty years it has held its own on the stage, and it will undoubtedly continue to do so for fifty more to come.

The reason isn't far to seek. The mystery play is the ideal form of numskull theatrical pleasure. The mystery of the theatre that once entranced the numskull has unfortunately disappeared for him, due to one thing and another, and the mystery that is currently lacking from the institution he finds in the mystery play itself. In place of the wonder of the stage that at one time enchanted his imagination, long since dissipated by nosey theatrical commentators, there is still for him, in such a play, the wonder of dramaturgic trickery. In place of the impenetrable secrets of behind-the-scenes that at one time challenged his curiosity, there is the dramatic secret to beguile his fancy. No longer is the hind pleasurably mystified, as once he was, by the theatre itself, so, hind that he is, he must find mystification for himself elsewhere. And find it he does in such exercises in occultism as trying to figure out which actor is the detective in disguise, which part of the painted canvas hides the sliding panel, and what caused the ominous ringing of the telephone bell the moment before the Hindu was found murdered in the library.

The theatre is successful with the mob in the degree that it is childish, and the mystery play is, of all forms of drama, the most childish. It perpetuates in dramatic form the favorite pastimes of childhood. It is a dramatization of such kid games as hide-and-seek, blind-man's-buff and finders-keepers. Instead of little Willie hiding behind the sofa and being discovered at length by little Salome, we have a grown-up actor dressed as a yeggman hiding behind a secret panel and being dragged out at length by another grown-up actor dressed as a policeman. Instead of a youngster with a handkerchief around his eyes stumbling over the parlor furniture in an attempt to seize the arm of another youngster and to identify him, we have an actor with a handkerchief around his common-sense stumbling through barriers arbitrarily interposed by the playwright in an attempt to seize and identify another character who has done something he hadn't oughter. And the youngsters in adult clothes out front are as awed by the nonsense as they were years ago when their big brothers first

241

persuaded them of hyperphysical gifts by asking them to turn around and, while their backs were turned, making a card magically disappear by the bafflingly mysterious device of saying Hocus-pocus-Henry-docus and sliding it into their pants' pockets.

§ 6

It is a practice of criticism to observe that the canvas of the stage is too small upon which to duplicate the tones and colors and crowded occurrences of any novel of considerable bulk. One hears the plaint when any novel of unusual length is turned into a play, when Thackeray, Dostoievski, Dreiser or even David Graham Phillips is set within the frame of the theatre. The job, on such occasions, is surely not an easy one, but I doubt, nonetheless, that the critical viewpoint is sound. The difficulty lies not with the canvas of the stage but with the dramatizer of the novel. He keeps the reader of the novel forever in his consciousness and addresses himself to that reader instead of to the auditor. Fearful of offending the reader, already familiar with the materials, by leaving out of the play any number of things that are wholly unessential to a dramatic interpretation of the novel, he produces a hybrid that is neither novel nor drama. The stage is amply capable of harboring the dramatization of any novel, however hefty, but it is not capable of harboring an unwieldy novel made into a play that aims to satisfy, at one clip, a spectator who is at once half-reader and half-auditor. Such a play fails because it attempts to jounce the theatre auditorium and synchronously to placate the library.

§ 7

One of the most depressing changes that has come about in the American theatre in our time is the gradual passing out of the old-time burlesque show, erstwhile delight of all connoisseurs of humor in its jockstrap. With the Columbia Wheel presently going in for revivals of "Uncle Tom's Cabin" and productions of such past Broadway successes as "White Cargo," with police injunctions to managers of such houses as the Chelsea either to behave or to shut up shop, and with the authorities of the Mutual Wheel toning down their exhibitions until they are indistinguishable from so many Epworth League picnics, the burlesque show as we knew it twenty years ago seems doomed to go the way of such other estimable American institutions as cock fights, rye whisky and liberty.

The signs of the death of burlesque have been in the air these last ten years and more. It was at about that time that the two hundred pound blondes whom once we frantically cheered began to send in coupons out of the backs of the magazines asking for free samples of reducing cream, that the sons of the late lamented house managers, succeeding to their fathers' posts after four years at Harvard, began to look askance at the scene in which Ludwig Dinkelplatz besought Hyman Finkelstein to take his feet out of the soup, and that the producers of the shows got rid of the old backdrop representing the Casino at Monte Carlo, a lovable standby since the Civil War, and bought in its place a second-hand set of scenery from the Casino at Broadway and Thirty-ninth street. It was also at this time that the burlesque entrepreneurs began to feel the first faint symptoms of morality and to wrinkle their brows over the scene in which the Irish comedian inquired ironically of Babe La Gervaise, the prima donna, why she wore her bustle in her shirtwaist, and why she wore two of them?

Up to this period, burlesque had been untrammeled and carefree. It was as left alone as a pretzel in Paris. And it flourished to the delight of all and sundry. Then came the first ripples of the blue waves that were presently to drown it, along with so many other things that once brought happiness to the humble American. Today, it is but a ghost of its former self, and that ghost is yearly getting more and more shadowy. Soon it will vanish completely. On the stage where once we boys applauded the spectacle of the great Al Reeves pointing to a blonde hippopotamus and asking if anyone in the audience would give him a quarter for her, provided he threw in his hat, there will be only a tenth-rate performance of some stale tenth-rate Broadway play. On the stage that once held "Krausmeyer's Alley," upon which no less than seven Presidents of the United States were fed in their youth, we shall hear nothing but the prayers of Little Eva. On the stage that once gave us, to our eternal joy, the money-changing act, the scene in which the German and Hebrew comedians pretended to be waiters in order to fool their wives and the scene wherein the Irish comedian got an eye full of flour when he talked into the telephone, we shall see nothing but a belated copy of the totem-pole number out of "Rose-Marie" and an imitation of the Tiller girls.

Not long ago, in a burlesque house down in Fourteenth street, I actually saw two sailors and a pickpocket break down and cry like children over the passing of the old order. The Hebrew comedian, instead of stealing up on the cooch dancer and jocosely belaboring her rear with a large bologna sausage, as in the happy days of the McKinley era, simply sidled nervously around her for a moment or two and made his exit. The Irish comique, instead of leaning under the table to get a better view of the soubrette's ample limb and falling on his nose as a result, simply went into a tame song and dance with the lady. And the German funny man, instead of sitting on the elephantine prima donna's lap and dropping nickels down her décolleté, approached the fair creature gingerly and bestowed a peck upon her shoulder-blade. To those of us who have the best interests of the native drama at heart and are willing to lay down our lives that the honor and integrity of the American theatre may be preserved, it was all too awful.

Speaking for the generation of the early '90's, I urge upon the burlesque impresarios a reconsideration of their present devastating and highly obnoxious plans. Let them give back to us Billy Watson in all his glory, together with the Heinies and Izzies and Mikes of blessed memory. Let them bring back, without delay, the old fat girls, the old floppy breeches, the old red undershirts, the old suspenders made of rope, the old green vests, the old Limburger cheese jokes, the old backdrop of Union Square, and the old scene in which the fierce-looking cop who cowed the comedians turned out to be a lizzie. Then again all of us Shakespeare and Ibsen enthusiasts will be happy.

§ 8

Anyone who watches the theatre closely cannot fail to note a periodic tendency on the part of producers to take an adult manuscript and attempt to give it youthful vitality by injecting into it the species of acting performances that mistake external exuberance of speech and deportment for an inner psychic glow. Unfortunately, this excessiveness of spirit that tries to counterfeit an inner enthusiasm fools no one. After the first half-hour, the bottom falls out and all that remains is an irritating disquiet. A feeling of freshness and life is not to be evoked by getting actors to act as if they were so many bouncing rubber balls, but rather by getting them self-effacingly to allow what freshness and life are in the play they are performing to ooze through them as through gauze. In the kind of melodrama that offers cardboard freight trains rushing through red gelatine forest fires and livery stable nags rupturing themselves on treadmills, the exuberant histrionic monkeyshines may be all very well, and they may be but slightly less appropriate to a certain kind of sofa-jumping farce, but when they are visited upon almost any other form of theatrical entertainment they puncture it and let the wind out of its sails.

§ 9

A lamentation over the absence of forthright

humor in the actors' performances usually follows any Gilbert and Sullivan revival as day follows night. Just what such critics mean, I have difficulty in making out. The Gilbert humor is a sly humor; it is designed to creep out through the proscenium arch, not to be shot out; it is satirical humor, not slapstick. It is, in short, a humor that envelops the play as a whole rather than a humor that enlivens it only periodically. It proceeds not so much from individual actors in the rôles of certain characters as from the group performance *in toto*. What the critics in question would seem to ask for is a species of performance that emphasizes certain portions of the humor at the expense of the humorous impression of the play as an entity.

There is no surer way to kill the humor of a Gilbert and Sullivan operetta than to merchant it through star clowns. One might as well play "The Importance of Being Earnest" with Clark and Mc-Cullough or "Cæsar and Cleopatra" with Ed Wynn and Fannie Brice. The Gilbert libretto and Sulli-van score humor is an ensemble humor; the moment the established zany tricks are brought into it its effect goes to pieces. The critics who deplore the absence of humor in such a case actually deplore not the absence of humor, for even they have more sense than that, but the absence of actor-comedy. What they want is not humor, but face-making and leg-shaking. What they demand is not humor but clowning. This is clearly to be seen in their habitual appraisals, specifically, of "Pinafore." They praise, and properly, the vaudeville performance of the rôle of Deadeye, the one minor clown rôle in the play, and then observe that it would be well for the other actors to take a cue from this particular actor. Deadeye is Gilbert's concession to the adult children in his audience, his Launcelot Gobbo, his servant to Olivia, his son to the reputed father of Perdita. He is no more the color of "Pinafore," light and gay though that color is, than the clowns of Shakespeare are the color of his comedies and dramas. The color of the humor of "Pinafore" is the light blue of its maritime backdrop. To deliver it in terms of a more commonplace theatrical humor is to devastate it. You can no more emphasize satire than you can emphasize an epigram in drawing-room

250

comedy. Yet that is precisely what the critics would appear to demand.

Gilbert and Sullivan, in the main, are best to be played with a complete lack of consciousness on the part of the mummers; the moment so much as one of them indicates that he thinks he is a rib-tickler the effect goes to pieces. I except, in this regard, one or two of the open and shut comedian rôles—the aforementioned Deadeye, for example, —but there exception ends.

§ 10

In the case of the periodic revivals of old plays it is not so much the old plays that are revived as the actors who appear in them. The managers get together a number of actors and actresses who were great favorites back in the days of high velocipedes and who haven't had a good job since Wallack's Theatre was torn down, herd them together on one stage, advertise them as "an all-star cast" and then delude themselves into believing that, because the actors are older and staler than the play, the latter will seem relatively new and fresh.

§ 11

One of the four or five thousand things that fails to work me up to a high pitch of indignation is the amount of money that the theatre ticket brokers charge for seats. It should be understood at the outset, of course, that there is no particular occasion for me to get mad about it, as I get all my seats for nothing. But, even if I were a paying customer, I have grave doubts that I'd stand up on my hind legs and yell when a broker charged me more for my tickets than the price printed on them.

It seems to me that the authorities, in their recent campaigns against the brokers, have operated with characteristic unfairness, which is a way that the authorities always have with them when it comes to the theatre. To demand that one be able to get one's tickets at the box-office window and without an advance in price is to demand that one be able to get one's suit at the Kuppenbaum factory and not be compelled to pay the added price asked by the suit brokers, or, in other words, the retail dealers. In almost all lines of trade there are middlemen, and the ticket brokers, as I look at it, are middlemen just the same as Gimbel, Saks and Rogers Peet. I'd like nothing better than to get my Gillette razor blades, for example, directly from the Gillette shop and so not have to lay out twenty-five or thirty cents more per package for them at the corner drug-store, but it apparently can't be done, although I'd be willing to buy them in fairly large lots. And so I no more can see why I should be able at any time to buy a dozen tickets for a theatre party at the Ziegfeld or Broadhurst or Belasco Theatre window and not have to pay a premium on them in one of the brokers' places of business. If I am compelled to pay a premium on my razor blades, why shouldn't I be compelled to pay one on my theatre tickets?

The theatre, however, is and always has been the patsy of district attorneys, federal attorneys, policemen, newspapers and almost everybody and everything else. When anyone in authority finds that he has a couple of hours hanging heavily on his hands and there is no one around to tell dirty stories to, he passes the time by kicking the theatre in the podex. He finds fault with the number of exits and fire-escapes, with the way tickets are disposed of, with the moral quality of the shows, with the Sunday night concerts, with the width of the aisles and passageways, with the age of the child actors, with the bareness of the girls' knees, with Mr. Erlanger's bookkeeper, Mr. Shubert's hat and a hundred other things. If the authorities ever ventured to bother Park and Tilford or Browning, King & Co. in the way they bother the theatre, those gentlemen would take them forcibly by the ear, lead them out into the back alley and rub their noses in dog-dirt.

But, for one reason or another, the theatre managers allow the authorities to pester them to death. If a manager has a good show and finds that, though all he asks for tickets is $3.85, the ticket brokers will gladly pay him a dollar apiece more for them, he permits the authorities to tell him that he has no right to take the extra dollar. If the brokers, in turn, can make another dollar or two profit on the deal, with the full and even eager concurrence of the club trade, and the authorities put them on the rack for doing exactly what any other good business men would do, the brokers curl their tails between their legs and take it lying down.

As I say, all this strikes me as very foolish. The brokers may occasionally swindle the boobs and suckers, but so do the lawyers, osteopaths, restaurant operators, orange-drink venders, correspondence school professors, hair-growing experts and half the shopkeepers of the land. Yet more often the brokers earn their profits. Let us say that you come to New York and have picked out, as the shows you wish to see, "Show Boat" and "The Spider," both big successes. You decide that you will have nothing to do with ticket brokers and will try to get your seats at the box-office. You are stopping, let us say, at the Vanderbilt Hotel. You take a taxicab and ride up to the Ziegfeld Theatre, get your tickets, and return to your hotel. With traffic conditions what they are, your taxi bill will in all probability be more than the extra fee a broker would charge you for your seats, and you are out considerable time, profanity and energy. And it will be the same if you try to penetrate the street jams and are compelled to obey the present

255

roundabout traffic regulations that will take your taxicab over to distant Eighth Avenue on your way to the Music Box. In addition, you will experience the discomfort of standing in line at the box-office window and the chance that the house is sold out and your trip will have been in vain. The brokers —all save two or three of the open-and-shut yegg-men—will get choice locations for you, will save you a lot of time, annoyance and taxi money and will send your tickets around to you so that you will not have to rush your dinner and get to the theatre ahead of time in order to claim them. If all that isn't worth an extra dollar or so, I am a very bad mathematician.

§ 12

Every time the gentlemen who pursue the art of journalistic moving picture criticism wish to deliver a dismaying blow to the gentlemen who strangely hold that the Guild Theatre, for example, is a source of somewhat greater pleasure to the civilized adult than one of Marcus Loew's cinema hash-houses, they point with a rich glee to some such play as "Creoles" and demand in a loud voice

256

where the latter gentlemen now get off. All of which tickles the Ignatz Goldfishes of the movies immensely. And all of which brings the rest of us to speculate why some one has never thought up the equally crushing argument that, because there are plaster-of-paris busts of Theodore Roosevelt, Michelangelo's "Slave" isn't much better than a sidewalk artist's drawing of a sunset in colored chalk.

§ 13

It was once a contention of the theatrical producers that the dramatic critics, most of whom actually knew little or nothing about the theatre, were concerned mainly with ruining their business. It has now become a contention of the dramatic critics that the theatrical producers, most of whom actually know little or nothing about the theatre, are apparently concerned mainly with ruining their own business. In support of this contention the critics point to a number of recent cases that show plainly how deficient certain of the producing gentry are in business sense, and how proud of that deficiency they seem to be.

If a manufacturer of razors were to name his

brand "The Always-Dull" or a purveyor of condiments were to employ a skull and cross-bones as his trademark, it might be reasonable to suspect him of certain cerebral failings. Yet we are asked to view theatrical producers as capable money-makers when they come forth with plays bearing such titles as "Sunshine" (with the subtitle, "A Comedy of Kindliness"), "The Adorable Liar," "First Love" and "Hearts Are Trumps." Any exhibit carrying a label like one of these is, in this late day of theatrical trade, doomed to be a loser before it starts. Even allowing for the considerable number of blockheads who still constitute the play-going public, it would take a practised optimist to figure out a profitable business for plays so christened. Some years ago such titles might have attracted the paying public; today, they simply frighten that public away, regardless of the quality of the plays themselves. The relish that the public once exhibited for such tender titles as "Lovers' Lane," "Little Orphant Annie," "Little Cream-puff," "My Dream Girl," "Sweet Iniscara," "Always-Cheerful Gladys" and even "Peg o' My Heart" has, one may believe, gone down the chute.

And today any billboard with a title like "Sunshine" on it simply calls for a horse-laugh. If the title is something like "The Little Spitfire," what proceeds is merely a yawn. Just what chance the producers of "Sunshine" and "The Little Spitfire" think they stand in a day when the crowds are attracted by titles like "Sex," "One Man's Woman," "The Great Temptations," "Cradle Snatchers," "Her First Affaire," ""The Virgin Man," "Sinner," "Crime" and "Her Cardboard Lover," is pretty hard to make out.

§ 14

Many years ago, I wrote of Ludwig Thoma's "Moral" and hinted that it might be a good idea for the theatrical managers of the time to produce it instead of such creachy tripe as "Daddy Dufard," "Everywoman," "Maggie Pepper" and "Strongheart," to which they were then with a whole heart devoting themselves. But, being then quite as sagacious as they are today and appreciating that if they produced the kind of plays I like they wouldn't have enough money on Saturday night to pay off the scrubwoman, they wisely paid no attention to me and astutely went on rolling up comfortable bank balances with gems like "The Governor's Lady," "The Bird of Paradise," "Stop Thief" and "Hawthorne of the U. S. A." With the passing of years, however, there came over the horizon a new order of producers. This new order shuddered at the very thought of making money. Rather than produce anything like "The Lion and the Mouse," "Alias Jimmy Valentine," "Arsène Lupin" or even McIntyre and Heath in "The Ham Tree" and contaminate themselves with filthy gold, they preferred to achieve a gravy of starvation, one collar a week and *kudos* with the sort of plays that were to the fancy of certain well-fed critics who had utterly nothing to lose and who very magnanimously allowed them to do all the dirty work and go hungry.

One set of these eminently worthy gentlemen, grouped under the name of the Actors' Theatre, not long ago dug back into my old files, saw therein mention of the Thoma play and proceeded to put it on. The production of the play was promptly made the occasion, on the part of a number of my colleagues, of considerable ironic comment at my expense. "What ho!" they observed, not without a measure of obvious self-satisfaction over their own sagacity in never having heard of the play; "Here is an opus highly recommended by the M. Nathan that yet plainly belongs to the theatre of yesterday and is now completely outdated!" That the charge made by my friends is more or less sound, I do not presume to deny. But equally sound would be the charge that Della Fox, whose good-looks I recommended at the same time I recommended "Moral," has dated even more. When I wrote of Thoma's play, it was a fresh and alive comedy with an original theme and with an original humor. In the years that have elapsed, a hundred and one playmakers have cabbaged not only its central idea, but most of its humor as well. In the last year or so alone we have had two steals from it: first, in certain of the comedy details which Molnar plus the Theatre Guild pilfered from its second act in order to brace up the scanty third act of "The Glass Slipper," and, secondly, in the theme and various embroideries of Lynn Starling's paraphrase called "Weak Sisters." And so it is that what was once a comedy that would have delighted the American theatre was, after these many years of neglect, properly found to be a wilted affair.

§ 15

The current favorite pastime of theatrical commentators is announcing the death of the road so far as dramatic entertainment goes and speculating upon the reasons. I myself have not been backward in joining in the sport, and have confected a number of essays upon the subject, rich in sapience. But although much that is unquestionably true has been written, many more things that are equally true have been omitted from the various disquisitions, and these may be worth a few moments' consideration.

Going back a couple of decades or so, we find that one of the cardinal articles in the American Credo was this: That all the managers of provincial theatres, before the Theatrical Syndicate reduced them to the status of janitors, were men with a lofty regard for art and, had they not been browbeaten and discouraged, would have played Shakespeare fifty-two weeks in the year, with Sophocles and Racine at matinées, instead of the Rogers Brothers, "Charley's Aunt" and Herrmann the Great. It was, these twenty and twenty-five years ago, the general belief that the road was being killed by the Syndicate, as if the Syndicate—even had it wished to with all its heart—could have regularly booked first-rate drama in the road theatres, when, as now, there was only one first-rate drama available for every two dozen or more second- and third-rate attractions. And, in addition, as I have implied, that the road theatre managers would have welcomed an uninterrupted diet of such first-rate drama with no chance of making a double amount of money out of bookings like "A Trip to Chinatown," Evans and Hoey's "A Parlor Match" (with Anna Held), and "Madeleine, or the Magic Kiss." This was the beginning of the legend that has persisted to the present day, and taken on, in passing, a wealth of new and peculiar blooms. The road was, and still is, held to have an overpowering itch for high dramatic art, when, as anyone at all familiar with the state of mind in most American provincial cities knows, the majority of first-

rate plays do not today and seldom in the past have
made enough money, save they were and are
trumped up with a popular star, to pay the week's
rent. What has brought about the death of the
road, unless I am losing my old cunning as a sooth-
sayer, has not been the shortage in reputable
drama so much as the shortage in spectacles, big
musical shows, mechanical melodramas and other
such stuff that once reaped a provincial harvest.
Send out today a "Miracle" or a "Scandals" or a
"The Spider" or any such thing and the road
promptly sits up in its grave and hands out its
money, just as it used to sit up in its then slightly
less deep grave and hand out its money for the
Hanlon and Yale and Byrne Brothers' spectacles,
or for the big Klaw and Erlanger musical shows,
or for Lincoln J. Carter and imported Drury Lane
melodramas. What we have today for provincial
export are chiefly only fifth-rate copies of first-
rate drama, chamber musical comedies and end-
lessly duplicated mystery melodramas with small
casts and innocent of sensational mechanical episodes, nine-tenths of which starve to death in New

York quite as they starve to death when they are sent out of New York. The road is in the condition it is for much the same reason that the New York theatre is in the condition it is. To believe the contrary is to believe that more than twenty (to be generous) out of the one hundred and eighty-odd plays and shows presented in New York last season made real money and, further, that the moving pictures are responsible for the road's staying away from such other one hundred and sixty-odd New York duds as "My Country," "Just Life," "Naughty Riquette," "Fanny," "The Wild Rose," "New York Exchange," "Money From Home," and the like.

If the road is in a bad way because of the dearth of what is euphemistically known as old-time first-rate drama, why is it in an equally bad way in the matter of big-time vaudeville? Surely that vaudeville is of a better grade today than it was fifteen and twenty years ago—one need only consider the greater number of competent legitimate actors and actresses who appear in its programs, to say nothing of the meritorious playwrights who now periodically contribute their one-act plays to it—and yet it has gone the way of the legitimate theatre and its offerings. I can't believe that the man in Pittsburgh, Cleveland, Philadelphia, Detroit, Chicago or St. Louis who used to patronize first-rate drama has suddenly become a great admirer of D. W. Griffith and Greta Garbo, or that the circumstance that his brother now owns a Ford and a radio keeps the latter, in turn, away from a leg show, provided the legs are good enough. The reason for the *Untergang* of the *Abendland* is not to be found, I believe, in any such facile and imbecile philosophy. The road has declined, in the directions in which it has done so, for other causes, a few of which I take the liberty of guessing at. In the first place, fully half the regular theatregoing element in the leading road cities now make periodic pilgrimages to New York and there see the good shows before they are presented in their respective towns. This was not true twenty years ago, when a trip to New York or anywhere else was something of an event. But the American of the class in point has come to be a great traveler in the intervening years; he leaves home on every possible occasion; and New York is his Mecca. A glance at railroad statistics will convince the doubter. And a glance at the statistics covering visitors to New York will convince him doubly. In the second place, the bookings of certain theatrical exhibits in the road theatres are for too long a period. In the old days, a play was booked for three nights or maybe a full week— the limit of the town's patronage. Today, a play of the same kind is booked for a much longer time and, naturally, plays to empty houses after its legitimately to be expected patronage is exhausted. In the third place, the so-called "try-outs" have alienated trade. Three-quarters of these try-outs are failures when finally they are brought into New York; they are swindles when foisted on the road by way of experiment; and the road gags at them quite as New York subsequently gags. And in the fourth place, to look at the other side of things, George Arliss, Ethel Barrymore, "Broadway" and the "Follies" do and perhaps always will have just as much success on the road as they have in New

York, while Pedro de Cordoba, Marjorie Rambeau, "Lily Sue" and "My Princess" will have no more and no less.

§ 16

While no more given to chauvinism than a Hoboken bartender, an American surveyor of the theatrical scene cannot help but think that without the American stage to give it life these days the English theatre would come very near having to shut up shop. This is true not only in the case of plays, but of productions, players, librettists, song writers, dancers, musicians, costume designers, monologists and even jokesmiths. What has brought about the collapse of a theatre that once, and not so very long ago, occupied an important position? What, with trivial exception, allows the clerks in the Keith-Prowse ticket agencies to snooze in their corners save the business in hand be to sell seats to imported American plays, shows and vaudeville acts? Theatrical London is today simply an American road town, hanging around in the doldrums until some second-rate American company comes along to awaken and to entertain it. With

the exception of an occasional talented Yankee
dramatic or musical comedy actress, we regularly
send over to England performers who are surely
anything but of the first order, yet these are received with the same indiscriminate favor as the
others. Actors who can't get jobs over here go
there and become overwhelming favorites. Actresses that no American producer will engage take
a boat and have to hire secretaries to turn down
offers. Singers confined over here to phonograph
records and the radio succeed in crowding the
London revue and vaudeville houses. Inferior pro-
dutions of New York shows get notices that the
English reviewers used to reserve for state occasions. With a single exception in the dramatic line,
musical comedy line and even vaudeville monologue line—a grand total of three—the American
performers in drama, musical comedy and vaudeville who have become the rage in London in
the last ten years have been given the bird in their
own land. Yet London has taken them to its bosom
with an undeviating affection. There are, true
enough, a few of the old English favorites who still
exercise their hold on the familiar London loyalty,

but the theatrical love-map is dotted profusely
with alien fly-specks. And today England pretty
uniformly pays out its money to cry with American
handkerchief moisteners, to laugh with American
comedians and to tap its feet in time with American trick pianists and tune manufacturers. It gets
its revue ideas from New York; its saxophone
blowers have to take lessons from American tutors
and then, having mastered their wind, for the pro-
tection of their own livelihood have to pass harsh
union laws keeping out of the country all American
musicians with more than one lung; its dramatic
theatres have to support scouts in New York to
ferret out plays that will keep their box-offices
open; its managers have to ally themselves with
American managers to get the benefit of the lat-
ters' judgment; its producers have to book west-
ward steamer accommodations at least three or four
times a season to inspect the local market and
fetch ideas back with them.

The trouble with the English theatre, I daresay,
is the trouble with the American moving picture:
both have come under a cloak and suit control.
Just as the American moving picture industry is

almost entirely in the hands of former pants makers, so is the English theatre of today almost entirely in the hands of former woolen merchants, butchers and coal dealers, the most of them hiding their identities and their prosaic pasts under the gauds of knighthood. There are more sirs in the English managerial ranks at the moment than the *maître d'hôtel* of the McAlpin grill greets in the round of a day's lunch. They are estimable fellows, no doubt, a bit ridiculous, perhaps, in the awkward wearing of still strange and far-fetched titles, but, equally without doubt, they are no more suited to theatrical management and production than so many drapers' clerks. They have money, much money, otherwise they would still be plain misters back in their old places of business, but they have no notion of what drama is and they have little taste, and so they seek to make a show for themselves by originating nothing and playing safe by acting as copycats. They do not know—how could they?—that there is material lying waste in England that might bring back to the English theatre a sense of the old native pride and glory. They do not know—for such news does not penetrate to woolen mills and butcher shops and coal depots—that beyond the Alps lies not only Italy but an Englishman named Craig whose genius has been banished from his homeland. They do not know—for such is vanity—that the art and the dignity of the theatre are no more to be entrusted to apostate tradesmen, even tradesmen in silk knee-breeches, than their American prototypes in the movie field know that the future of the pictures, if forsooth it is conceivable that the pictures have one, is to be vested in apostate mink peddlers and dill pickle dealers.

§ 17

The mood of indignation tends gradually to disappear from the drama. Just as somebody or other invariably named Horwitz seems always to be writing indignant letters to the *Nation,* so in days past were dramatists habitually given to writing plays wholesale in resentment of this and that. It takes no veteran to remember the time when the bulk of drama, both good and bad, was not so much *for* something as *against* something, and when the opposition was couched in terms that clearly betrayed the playwright's animosity, no less than the animosity of the audiences he catered to. With the increasing sophistication of dramatic writers and theatre audiences, the era of huff has begun to fade, and the drama of today, as a consequence, is generally found to be one of relative equanimity and composure.

The theory that a dramatist must, because of the very nature of his medium, feel strongly if he would sway his audiences may be sound enough if one visualizes his audiences as a pack of dolts, but, with audiences somewhat worthier, it is a better theory that he must rather think strongly and then set about cautiously to filter his thought through characters who at least have the air of being nonchalant toward his conclusions. That the drama is fundamentally emotional may be true enough, but the definition has been manhandled out of all sense. There are many kinds of emotion, yet the definition coddlers almost uniformly think of just two: love and hate, conveniently overlooking the fact that some of the finest drama deals with emotions vastly more trivial, emotions that may be said, indeed, to be almost negative emotions and that often are far removed from the heart and the spleen. The best comedy written in France in the present century is founded entirely upon the emotion of physical irritation; one of the best comedies that has come out of Ireland in the same period is founded entirely upon the emotion of pleasurable self-gullery; the drama of Shaw, with small exception, is as unemotional as a mushroom, as is some of the best of Pirandello. But all this is somewhat beside the point. The point is that high emotion and the so-called taking of sides are bed-fellows, and that indignation is their child. As high emotion has been relegated to the background in drama, the taking of sides has retreated into the background with it and indignation has accordingly vanished.

The drama of today does not *tell* its audience something; it suggests to the audience that the latter may judge of what it says for itself. It gives it sly hints on the way, to be sure, but it no longer, in the aggregate, looks the audience straight in the eye and tells it to go to Heaven. The moralist tone has vamoosed, and so, too, has the index finger of admonition and warning. There is a soothing moral and philosophical *double entente* in the case of the former heroes and villains, and audiences are permitted to feel for themselves even if they are not always permitted to think for themselves. The stage gutter is no longer full of wayward women; gentlemen with black moustaches and sleek evening coats no longer inevitably end up either at Sing Sing or Frank Campbell's; blond bravos do not regularly marry their bosses' daughters; and capital and labor often come to decisionless dog-fall. Pistols are relegated to 10–20–30 melodrama, and handcuffs have passed out with Houdini. There used to be two sides to every question, unless it were a dramatic one. That is changed now. So great has the change been, indeed, that the drama of to-day not only presents the two sides but periodically, as in the instance of something like Maugham's "The Constant Wife," generously and open-mindedly presents three!

Strong feeling is too often the mark of a weak dramatist. The inferior man, in whatever field his labors lie, is chronically an indignant one. There is small place for indignation in art. The Eroica, let us remember, was finished before its composer's momentary wrath caused him to change its title; nor was it surely save deliberately that the greatest tragic dramatist of all time put many of his most indignant speeches in the mouths of his clowns. The boiling acerbity of Strindberg has to-day become the material of light comedy and farce, and the passionate alarms of French problem plays find less and less favor even in France where, year by year, the Guitrys and Armonts and Gerbidons wean more and more customers away from the Batailles and Bernsteins and Hervieus. Sex, the chief ground of dramatic indignations of the past, has become theatrically largely a laughing matter, or if not precisely a laughing matter, most often a casual one. Even the occasional boob-bouncer that seeks diligently to go after the old trade with the Jones and Pinero sex furors finds it necessary to add at least a sensational murder or some such circus-act to the business if it would effectively diddle its audiences. It is clearly thus that a "Mrs. Dane's Defence" of the earlier dispensation becomes a "The Letter" and that Iris Bellamy becomes Iris March. Wedekind, in his louder sex moments, is now snickered at even by the Germans and what prosperity he still enjoys is at the hands of Berlin Greenwich Villagers still wet behind the ears. Hauptmann, sensing the change, abandons sex and turns to theology. Even the philosophical Elinor Glyn, Sudermann, waxes sardonic. Across the border, Donnay turns to satire and ironic comedy and the erstwhile paprika-schnitzel, Brieux, to economics and international amity.

Following the tendency of drama, stage direction has naturally come also to pacify itself. So far, indeed, has this direction gone that even where the drama still shows traces of indignation it exerts itself to the utmost to conceal the fact. Even a murder in this day is staged something after the manner of a petting party, and loud voices are confined to musical comedy. Fifteen and twenty years ago, a play was regarded as dramatic in proportion to the racket it made; climaxes were indistinguishable from college yells and evangelical sermons. Actors like the late James K. Hackett and John Mason, who could shiver the ceiling with bull roars, were never out of jobs, and stage directors without megaphones were as rare as movie directors without puttees and polo shirts. All this is no more. The stage of today, by and large, discharges its drama through a muffler; the old trombone has a derby hitched to its snout. There are, of course, virtues to the new order, but one cannot help feeling that there are also weaknesses. The thing has been carried too far. It is all very well for a certain species of drama to be staged *piano,* but there is surely another species that may be staged thus only at the expense of absurdity. Yet melodrama and drawing-room comedy are often produced in an identical fashion, with the result that the theatre is growing monotonous. The so-called natural, life-like type of staging is taking the inherent bounce out of many an otherwise popping play. Too much naturalness is as bad for the theatre as too much theatricality is bad for life. A toy bear that growls and walks when wound up is all right, but one that would also bite one in the leg wouldn't do at all. The theatre, too, is a toy and, like a toy, though it may well improve itself, should remain more or less the plaything it is and not try to make itself indistinguishable

278

from the actuality it merely and properly pretends to be.

§ 18

Something will have to be done pretty soon about this business of intermissions. Although the theatre has bettered itself in many directions in recent times, it has, with negligible exception, overlooked its perhaps most senseless and damaging shortcoming, to wit, the custom of interrupting a play at two or more intervals during its course, sending the audience out into the lobby on furloughs and messing up beyond repair both the audience's mood and the even tenor of the play. An example is to be had in the instance of such a thing as the Theatre Guild's production of the dramatization of "Porgy." Here we had what might have been an interesting dramatic exhibit almost totally ruined by three long intermissions, to say nothing of six shorter ones between scenic adjustments. Each of these pauses in the dramatic narrative acted as a wet blanket both upon the narrative itself and, even more so, upon the audience, for it was only by a severe self-imposed strain that the audience managed to recover its several moods once they had been doused out of activity by the breaks in the play's flow. The net impression of the evening, consequently, was of a series of intermissions periodically interrupted by a play, and when such an impression works its influence upon an auditorium no genius on earth can send an audience out into the night either fully persuaded or satisfied.

It is high time, it seems to me, that this foolish tradition as to the necessity of *entr'actes* be seized by the tail and got rid of. The theory that an audience's attention must be given periodic respites and that an audience asked to exercise its faculties for two straight hours without rest would gradually become weary and offer a poor percussion, is, I dare say, quite as hollow as most theories that cling like barnacles about the theatre. Even a moving picture audience, the lowest form of audience conceivable, willingly—even enthusiastically—sits at rapt attention for something like two straight hours at the so-called feature film productions displayed in the Broadway theatres. And if such morons can manage the business I can see no reason why the intelligent audiences that the Theatre Guild and the better grade producers cater to cannot be expected to do the same. The tremendous heterogeneous crowds that patronize professional baseball sit calmly for hours with their eyes glued to the rapidly shifting and often trying play on the diamond and, save for a moment's stretch in the seventh inning, never relax their absorption or their bottoms. Yet the theatre believes that when these same people come into it to watch a play that begins at quarter to nine and ends at quarter to eleven, a period of two short hours, it is necessary to give them at least two substantial periods of truce.

The intermission idea is all very well in the case of musical shows, where the audience's mood and the show's continuity are not impaired by it, but in the case of drama it makes, save on rare occasions, for disaster. If a movie audience can stand the two-hour screen version of "What Price Glory?" without let-up, surely a theatre audience should be able to stand the two-hour version of the same play in the same way. That it can stand it and will stand it gladly, to its own greater enjoyment and to the greater prosperity of the dramatic manuscript, our impresarios will soon discover if they give it the chance. Many a play that now goes to pieces during the intermissions will thus gain an added quality of coherence, evenness and interest, and many an audience that presently doesn't know why it is that it gradually loses concern with a play will quickly be conscious of the nature of its previous difficulty.

§ 19

A playwright should be ever mindful of the fact that stage realism, even at its best, is always more or less dubious and ridiculously artificial. All that one need do to appreciate the essential absurdity of stage realism is to observe what it looks like when photographed. There never was a realistic scene or a realistic dramatic episode that didn't comically go to pieces when you looked at it on a lobby-stand.

§ 20

The student of theatrical affairs must rapidly come to the conclusion that French farce has become a pretty dead thing outside of France, where the trite and stale have a habit of enjoying long life. Almost all the French farces that have been produced in America, England and Germany in the last seven or eight years have come croppers. For one that has modestly succeeded, due to the appearance in it of some public pet, a half-dozen have failed. And the failures have been so abrupt that one is brought to speculate as to the causes.

There was a time, not so many years ago, when French farce prospered outside its own country, and when French farce writers could look to foreign markets for substantial royalty returns. Today, it becomes increasingly evident that these markets are getting to be extremely cold and that a completely arctic temperature is in sight. As to the reasons, I offer a few guesses. In the first place, American, English and German theatrical managers have almost invariably during the last decade imported the least original and least meritorious of the Gallic farces, neglecting entirely those manuscripts that might revive and stimulate the waning interest in this particular form of stage fare. Among the many amusing farces produced on the boulevards in the last fifteen years, I can't think of more than two that have been produced in any one of the three countries named. The farces that have been produced have been of the second, third and even tenth cut, without novelty, without kick, without quality of any kind. The best work of such expert farce writers as Guitry, Dieudonné, Mazade and Coolus has been neglected, and only the uninspired hack work of the rubber-stamp boys displayed to the alien gaze. It was not long, therefore, before alien audiences began to grow tired of the same old door-banging, bed-bouncing rigmarole and before they withdrew their trade.

In the second place, a change has come over thitherward audiences in a sex direction. There was a time when the sex didos of the French farce writers seemed very saucy and juicy, but today they have come to take on an air of conventionality, and not only of conventionality but, I dare say, of relative innocence. The so-to-speak more serious drama has gone so far with sex themes that the French farces, even at their naughtiest, begin to seem tame. What French farce in the last half-dozen years, for example, has gone farther with sex than such a play as "The Captive," or "Women Go On Forever," or "Bride of the Lamb," or "Seed of the Brute," or—to speak of farces—the German ones called "The Werewolf" or "The Command To Love"? The days when a French sex farce seemed to a British or American audience something like a visit to a peep-show have disappeared down the hole of time. Not a single scene in any one of these farces produced in America in the last ten years has brought so pleasurable a blush to the boob cheek as the nymphomaniac episode in "The Shanghai Gesture," the scene between the clergyman and Sadie Thompson in "Rain," or the confession scene in "The Trial of Mary Dugan." And not one of the French farces has gone farther in a loud sex direction than fifty such locally exhibited dramatic affairs as "No More Women," "Gentle Grafters," "Creoles," "Scotch Mist," "An American Tragedy," "The Firebrand," "The Pearl of Great Price," "This Was a Man," "Sex," "The Virgin Man," "Pinwheel," "A Lady in Love," "A Very Wise Virgin," and so on. And in Germany, the naughtiest French farce imaginable takes on the aspect of an ice-cream festival beside such dramatic works as "Reigen," "Erdgeist" and "Vatermord."

With the sex bait diminished, the French farce writers find themselves in sore straits. But very few of them are really witty fellows and these few have been discouraged by the chilly attitude toward them of American and English entrepreneurs. Until their farces are produced in America and in England—and in Germany—French farce must remain in abeyance so far as these audiences are concerned.

§ 21

The man who makes a business of criticism, as other men make a business of house-wrecking and sewer-repairing, is a natural target for all persons, lay and professional, who resent his presumption in electing himself judge of them and of their presumptions in turn. Among these critics of critics, one finds at times fellows gifted with considerable penetration and artful in detecting defects, for the smoothest of critics, like the smoothest of apples, are not always entirely free from worms. But, more often, we find the kind of persons who, though they

286

are as strange to logic as a cat to catsup, yet arbitrarily feel themselves in duty bound to hand something to critics, whatever it is. They are annoyed by critics; they do not like them; and they are ready with a *timbale* of custard to answer the call to war.

There has never been a critic of anything, high or low, who has not suffered the pastry of the anti-critical forces. In times gone by, this pastry took the form of hemlock or the Bastille. Today, it takes the form of loud cussing, slander, innuendo and comprehensive and general personal abuse and detraction. A critic like Shaw is charged with knowing nothing about women because he is a vegetarian and hence, unlike a man given to Hamburg steaks and pork chops, lacking in *pruritus genitalium*. A critic like Max Beerbohm is sniffishly waved aside because he is anatomically at one with Zipporah's son and because he is bald-headed. A critic like Friedrich Brie is viewed as if he himself had commanded U-boat 35, and one like Frank Harris is summarily dismissed on the ground that they don't do such things in any respectable Sunday School, at least during school hours. Henri

Béraud is put to rout with whispers that he wears pink underdrawers, and it is argued against the lately lamented Georg Brandes that once, in his youth, he was seen treating a pretty ballet dancer to an *Eisschokolade*. Times change, indeed, but little, and then only in the degree of attack. Castelvetro was given a black eye by Caro; Ben Jonson was driven to the extreme of fighting a duel with a man who objected to his criticism; Lessing was denounced frequently as a *Schnapps* addict; Goethe was said to be beneath the notice of respectable Germans because of his carryings-on with the fair Vulpius; Sarcey, it was ironically gabbled about, was as partial to the well-made women of the boulevards as he was to the well-made plays of Scribe and Sardou; Nietzsche, with much significant head-tapping, was declared to be suffering from the effects of lewd cocci; and, to drop in two senses to nearer days, James Gibbons Huneker was declared to be a critic who couldn't be accepted because of the obvious Teutonic genesis of his surname and Stuart Pratt Sherman because of the equally obvious implications of his middle.

Of all periods in which criticism of critics has flourished, the immediate present is, however, undoubtedly the greatest. Critic-baiting has become an even greater and more typical American sport than framing prize-fights or fixing horse-races and championship baseball games. The man who practises professional criticism in this Year of Our Lord lives constantly in a metaphorical gas-house district, his head and seat in imminent prospect of bash and boot. I surely do not mean to defend critics, for Heaven knows that many of them deserve all that they get, and more. For what Hazlitt wrote of the hack writer only too patly may be written of a recognizable share of his modern prosecutors. The estimable William's words I recall to you: ". . . He thinks his not understanding your drift exceedingly droll and laughable; blunders again, and, when he discovers his mistake, fancies he has you at an advantage. He picks up a lie or a sophism and repeats it with hireling pertness and gravity, for the benefit of clergy, gentry and the respectable part of the community who are readers of ———. In shuffling off an objection, he first reduces it to his own standard of meaning

289

and then answers it very wisely. His happy in-
capacity admits just so much of an idea as leaves
no thought and no feeling. . . . By natural as-
similation, whatever his pen touches turns to wordy,
nauseous impertinence, and to convict him of a
breach of probity or make him ashamed of a lie
it would be necessary to endue him with a new
faculty, and to let him see that there is anything
in the world of the slightest importance that is not
a mere bagatelle, but as it furnishes matter for his
interest, servility, callous foppery, pertness and
conceit." But, unfortunately, it is not the custom
of the critic-baiter to distinguish between com-
petence and incompetence on the part of his hated
one, and he indiscriminately lets fly to right and
left. The circumstance that the fellow is a critic is
enough.

MAGNUS MAXIMUS

Preceded by that species of irrelevant and trumpery press-agency which, somewhat disconcertingly, he would seem fond of allowing to make him appear rather like German silver, Max Reinhardt, the foremost active producer in the world theatre, has lately come again across the Atlantic to display his wares. That this virtuoso of dramatic production should permit himself publicity devices that Peaches Browning and even Otto Kahn might balk at is gagging to those of his critics who peculiarly believe that art and dignity should have something in common and who have difficulty in determining just what connection there can be between some of the very finest dramatic presentations of the modern stage and a lot of free lunches at Salzburg, to say nothing of widely disseminated photographs showing the impresario and Miss Julia Hoyt posed against the façade of Schloss Leopoldskron eating sizeable hunks of *Wiener Lungenbäuscherl*. For while such stuff may be all right on the part of self-advertising vaudeville actors and pentecostal clergymen it is hardly an admirable business for a man of Reinhardt's attainments. He may thus impress a senate of doodles, but in the minds of others he lowers himself considerably.

That Reinhardt is the most talented director and producer operating in the theatre in these years is certainly not news, except perhaps to a few Russians. With Craig, the greatest genius of them all, in forced retirement in Genoa, with Stanislavsky, a skilful fellow, calmly relying for eminence upon a few already ancient achievements, with Dantchenko, very little better than a second-rater, idiotically frittering away his time out in Hollywood and with Pitoëff going in simply for a series of exaggerated imitations and caricatures in France, Reinhardt has the field pretty well to himself. He is an extraordinarily fertile and alive figure, indefatigable, imaginative and resourceful; he works like a Trojan; he has, unlike these other producers, a sense of internationalism—all drama, whatever the land of its origin, is of interest to him; he has a mind that adapts itself to a diversity

292

of drama and a fancy that filters it with a various force and beauty onto a fluid and galvanic stage. It is Reinhardt's outstanding characteristic indeed, and the quality that has raised him to leadership among the active producing talents of the day, that he is, in a sense, a different man in the instance of each separate production which he makes. Where the majority of producers have a very definite and unmistakable personal label that sticks betrayingly to each of their presentations, however essentially different the dramas themselves may be, Reinhardt changes his directing personality according to the drama he happens to be dealing with. There is not one director Reinhardt—there are a dozen director Reinhardts. But there is only one Stanislavsky, one Gemièr, one Granville Barker, one Copeau or one Sierra, be the play farce or comedy, tragedy or allegory, spectacle or what not. The signature is genuine, but the contents of the bottle are often spurious. For these directors and others like them are bent upon impressing their own idiosyncratic personalities on a variety of drama where Reinhardt is concerned chiefly with so adjusting the many facets of his directorial per-

sonality that that one of them that most patly suits
the particular drama in hand shall not obscure the
latter to his own vainglory and to its own infinite
damage.

Going into the theatre of any outstanding director and producer save Reinhardt, one can discern the director's arbitrary method and technique,
be the exhibit Shakespeare or Racine, Lenormand
or Oscar Wilde. The label is there as flamboyantly
—and as dubiously—as on a bottle of bootleg
Scotch. Everything is sacrificed to make a Roman
holiday for the producer himself, and for his personal *kudos*. The dramatist is simply a tool wherewith he seeks to fashion his own monument. Among
directors both big and little the world over one finds
this vain adherence to and exposition of an inflex-
ible technique or style, as set in each of its several
ways as the writing tricks of the more celebrated
popular fictioneers or the steps of the more celebrated colored hoofers. Thus, one need not refer
to the playbill to know a Stanislavsky production,
whether of Tchekov or Maeterlinck: the Stanislavsky idiosyncrasies periodically thrust themselves
forward willy-nilly, and the devil take the drama-

tist. So, also, with Jessner—at times, like Stanislavsky, a praiseworthy craftsman—and his arbitrary
stairways, with Copeau and his arbitrary salon
method of staging, with Pitoëff and his arbitrary
bolshevik hocus-pocus, with Gemièr and his arbitrary portière nonsense, with Barker and his arbitrary gilt Oxonianism, with Arthur Hopkins and
his arbitrary Barnowski naturalism or—to descend
to the little fellows—with Belasco and his silk
laboriously thrown over cotton, Basil Dean and his
drugstore-window-lighting monkeyshines, and the
relatively much superior André and his second-
hand Reinhardtisms out of Rapallo.

In Reinhardt's theatre, as I have noted, technique
of production is no such more or less exactly
pigeonholed business. For each separate drama a
new technique is devised. For one, we have the
Craig concepts visualized by the Reinhardt imagination; for another, the principles of the Com-
media del'Arte elaborated and edited; for still
another, music and the spoken word deftly orches-
trated; for still another, the Sixteenth Century
moralities beautified by a Twentieth Century looking imaginatively backward; for yet another, mod-

ernism plus modernism; and for yet another still, impressionism and expressionism enjoying a picnic of acutely critical production. In this lies the estimable and protean Max's directorial expertness and felicity: that all manner of drama is grist for his mill and that, more important, that mill revolves not to a single wind, as with the other producers, but to whatever wind the drama in point may blow. There are times, it may be, when Reinhardt plainly strains himself for effect, when a trace of illegitimacy insinuates itself into his work and causes one transiently to suspect the mountebank, when those snapshots of Max kneeling piously before a ten-foot crucifix in Schloss Leopoldskron with Fanny Brice, Morris Gest and other such devout fellow Christians come to mind, but in the general run of things the honest artist is clearly to be felt and seen beneath and beyond the momentary posturer. Reinhardt, with Papa Craig peeping over his shoulder, has brought more actual life to the modern stage than any other practising director and producer of his time. His influence has spread over all lands and seas. He has been Gordon Craig's Paul.

A NOTE ON THE TYPE IN
WHICH THIS BOOK IS SET

This book is composed on the Linotype in Bodoni, so-called after its designer, Giambattista Bodoni (1740–1813) a celebrated Italian scholar and printer. Bodoni planned his type especially for use on the more smoothly finished papers that came into vogue late in the eighteenth century and drew his letters with a mechanical regularity that is readily apparent on comparison with the less formal old style. Other characteristics that will be noted are the square serifs without fillet and the marked contrast between the light and heavy strokes.

SET UP, ELECTROTYPED AND PRINTED BY
THE VAIL-BALLOU PRESS, INC.,
BINGHAMTON, N. Y.
ESPARTO PAPER MANUFACTURED
IN SCOTLAND, AND
FURNISHED BY W. F. ETHERINGTON & CO.,
NEW YORK.
BOUND BY H. WOLFF ESTATE,
NEW YORK.